MOUNTAIN BIKING ADVENTURES

》 ABOUT US

MB7 has grown out of the buzzing mountain biking scene in southern Scotland. We're based in the Tweed Valley, 20 miles south of Edinburgh, on the doorstep of Glentress Forest.

Our philosophy is simple - to ensure as many people as possible can experience our trails by offering courses and holidays which take in the best on offer in our local area.

》 FIND OUT MORE

Take advantage of our local knowledge to explore the best man-made & natural singletrack of 7stanes country.

web 》 WWW.MB7.COM
email 》 RIDE@MB7.COM
phone 》 08706 093 096

Selected mountain bike rides in Southern Scotland & the 7stanes

First Edition

By

Ali Chant, Sue Savege, Iain Withers

Illustrations

Andrew Lai, Ali Chant

ISBN: 0-9549762-8-2

Cover photo

Route: McMoab Kirroughtree. Rider: Ali Chant. Photographer: Sue Savege

Publisher's note:

Mountain bike routes are subject to the forces of both nature and man, and can change on a day to day basis. Every effort has been made in putting together this book to check routes and ensure the accuracy of the mapping. But beware rain can wash out the trail, forest routes can come and go and routes seem to get harder or easier in direct proportion to the amount of time spent in the saddle. Make sure you are ready for your day out in the dirt and check out the latest updates on access and trail conditions at www.bike-fax.com.

This book includes mapping data licensed from Ordnance Survey

Published by Bikefax Ltd. North Wales. UK. www.bike-fax.com
© Copyright 2006 Bikefax Ltd. MB7 Coast to Coast © Copyright MB7 2006

Contents

Southern Scotland & the 7stanes

The Final Cut

First came the fun part. We spent months on a voyage of discovery throughout southern Scotland, riding every track going. We rode all of the fast and furious 7stanes routes, had our multi-day epics and bothy visits, discovered that you could still be hard-core on natural trails in the Galloway hills and clocked up well over a 1000 kilometres of riding on everything from mountain to moor, forest trails to coastal rambles and DH to XC.

Then, after all this, came the hard bit, choosing which of all the outstanding rides should go into the guide. This was no easy task, as we all loved each and every trail we had ridden, and with so much variety in the area, we found it desperately hard to leave anything out. In the end, with the help of the opinions and suggestions of a lot of well informed locals, we had to make the final cut and leave the rest for volume 2.

No doubt the final selection will be hotly debated and the adventurous rider will already be out finding variations of their own, but we're confident that the dozens of routes described in this guide will keep most riders busy for quite a while yet!

How to use this guide

As mountain bikers, we've often thought about what we would want from a guidebook ourselves. We all know how difficult it is to turn up in a brand new area and not know quite where to start, hence this guide. With the help of local riders, we've done some of the work for you, checking out the local services and riding the trails with notebook, camera and GPS, to put together the best information possible.

To make it easy for riders to choose the right route, the routes have been arranged by geographic area, with each area then giving a selection of routes at a variety of grades. If you want to find all the downhill, cross country, epics etc in the region, have a look at the 'Graded List' at the back of the book.

Maps & Symbols

The maps used in this guide are based on standard Ordnance Survey mapping. The maps have then been redrawn to highlight the most important information whilst giving mountain bike riders additional detail to help with getting the most out of the ride.

Whilst we have made every effort to check the accuracy of our maps, there are times when only a full detailed map will do and for the longer, more remote rides we strongly recommend that you take a map and compass with you- and know how to use them!

Icons

The icons on the map should give you extra information about the nature of the trail, as well as the location of any amenities such as bike shops and cafes, that you might find en route.

Gradings explained

The gradings in this book are here for you to decide what's your own poison: ride with the challenge of never 'dabbing'; push yourself on something a little harder than usual, or stay well within your comfort zone.

It is notoriously hard to grade the level of difficulty of mountain bike routes. So much will depend on you, the bike and the conditions on the day. As well as this, the level of difficulty of a route can change from year to year, as tracks get washed out by the rain, maintained or rebuilt.

In this book we attempt to give you some guide as to the level of the hardest riding to expect on each route. Remember though it is only a guide.

This guide contains both 'Downhill' (DH) tracks and classic 'Cross-Country' (XC) rides.

Downhill Routes - DH

Downhill routes are given a technical grade from 1 to 5 to indicate their level of severity and technical difficulty.

The higher the grade: the harder the route. All this means higher grades equal bigger jumps, steeper inclines and more demanding technical sections.

 Easy

Straightforward off-road riding, mainly on forest roads and wide grassy tracks. All you need is some knobbly tyres on your bike and you can go for it. Suitable for all including novices and children.

Moderate

Wide bumpy trails with a choice of lines, simple singletrack, moderate inclines and nothing too technical.

③ Hard

Fast flowing singletrack, with generally good traction on the surface. Good bike control needed and some quick decision making. Expect variable surfaces from smooth hardpack to loose rock, mud and roots. Small jumps and rollers.

④ Extreme

Technically challenging riding with tight switchbacks, narrow rutted tracks and loose surfaces. Fast riding with jumps, steep inclines and obstacles all around you. Riding where expert bike control is essential and good balance at a premium. On DH tracks at least wear elbow and shin pads on this stuff.

⑤ Off the Scale

Big jumps, scary landings, impossible surfaces and split second decision making. You'll most likely be wearing full body armour for this stuff. Limited or no chicken runs here. Routes for those who 'have it' on a regular or competition basis.

If you don't find these rides hard – turn pro!

Cross Country Rides - XC

Cross-Country rides use a dual grading system to indicate both the nature of the ride and the hardest level of technical difficulty which you are likely to encounter.

First of all the overall grades, ranging from 'Epic to Family', give you a general impression of the route, then numeric 1 – 5 grades, give you an idea of the technical difficulty of the ride. Put the two gradings together, for example, Expert 3 to get the real impression what to expect on a cross country ride.

Epic

Epic routes, as the name implies, can contain serious sections of downhill for long periods of time, or thigh-ripping technical uphill, or both! These rides will present some severe endurance issues! Go prepared as anything can come at you at anytime.

Expert

Almost wholly off-road. You'll need a reasonable level of fitness and a fair bit of experience on a bike. Riding on these trails can be of a challenging nature and you'll be trying your best not to fall off.

Classic

With big sweeping views and good distance coverage these rides can take you far from the beaten track. Classic routes will appeal to the rider who wants to cover the miles, see the scenery and enjoy the ride.

Blasts

Blow away the cobwebs when you've only got an hour or so to spare or for when the weather is being particularly ugly in the mountains. These routes offer a quick up and down, but don't underestimate them, some of these little routes can pack a powerful punch.

Family

Mountain biking isn't just for the grown ups, start 'em young and get the kids out on the bikes too. Family rides combine short easy rides with an element of fun. Easy riding on wide tracks mean that these routes are just as suitable for novices as they are for the kids.

Kit and Equipment

Cross Country

If you're going off the beaten track or into the high mountains, it's a good idea to take a few extra bits with you.

- Spare food & clothing
- Spare clothing
- First Aid
- Hydration
- Couple of spare tubes each
- Repair kit/Multi-tool
- Zip Ties & Gaffer tape (you can temporarily fix just about anything with these)
- Mobile Phone - Be aware that you may not be able to get a signal in some places
- A well maintained bike
- Local map and compass

Downhill

You'll most likely be going downhill pretty steeply and, pretty fast, often through some very tight tree sections on these routes, so we recommend that you pad yourself up as well as possible.

- Full gloves
- Full face helmet (never go on DH trails without at least a normal mtb helmet)
- Long sleeves
- Full body armour if you've got it
- Elbow guards
- Knee and shin pads at least
- Backguard, ideally
- Chainguard (to protect your bike)

Code of Conduct

General common sense applies here of course. The age-old rule of 'show consideration to others and they'll be considerate to you', works on the whole. For all the times that this doesn't work, a basic minimum of politeness should at least mean that we present a positive image of our sport.

- Always ride on legal trails
- Leave no trace
- Be sensitive to the soil beneath you and practice low-impact cycling.
- Stay in control of your bike
- Always give way to faster riders on DH. On XC give way to riders coming up the hill.
- Let your fellow trail users know you're coming. Anticipate other trail users around corners or in blind spots
- Never scare animals
- Leave gates as you found them, or as marked
- Plan ahead and be self sufficient

What to do in an emergency

If it does all go horribly wrong and someone in your group ends up in a big bloody pile on the floor, then this is where all that extra stuff comes in handy. First of all make sure your casualty and everyone else for that matter stays warm, get him or her in to shelter and patch 'em up if you can.

If they're too crook to walk out, it's probably time to call for some help. If you are in the forest, they might be able to get the ambulance to you, anything more remote and it's going to be a job for the Mountain Rescue.

The number to call from your mobile is 112, or 999 on a landline. Ask for the police, explain your situation, try to tell them exactly where you are (FC routes often have numbered posts to identify your location) and the nature of the injuries, and they will then call the appropriate services.

Remember to keep the phone on after this, as they will need to get back to you for more details. Then sit back and wait; it could easily be a couple of hours before someone can get help to you.

The moral of the story is RIDE SAFE, take plenty of kit and 'don't crash and burn'.

When someone first came up with the idea of linking 7 Scottish forests with a set of iconic mountain bike trails and thus creating the 7stanes project, they couldn't have known what pure genius there was laying dormant in their idea. The vision of creating a world class mountain biking venue has realised itself in the 7stanes and lucky old us in the UK for having it right on our doorstep.

The 7stanes is definitely the new wave of riding here in the UK. The miles of hand crafted singletrack to be found at centres like Mabie and Glentress will have you floating down the trail like a God.

Boulder pavements, evil rock gardens and tricky technical teasers can be found in abundance at Kirroughtree and Dalbeattie, and downhillers will love the sweet, full bounce tracks at Ae and Innerleithen. Families haven't been forgotten either with more gentle ride options at Glentrool and Newcastleton. In this guide we have highlighted a selection of what we consider to be the finest trails in the 7stanes, but at the end of the day it's a personal selection. And a hard selection to make too – 'cos they're all so darned good...

Dalbeattie

Iron Hash Trail...................... **1** XC
Moyle Hill Trail.................... **2** XC
Hardrock Trail...................... **3** XC

Tweed - Glentress

Skills Loop........................... **1** XC
Buzzards Nest...................... **2** XC
The Hub.............................. **2** XC
Glentress Red...................... **3** XC
Helly Hansen V Trail........... **4** XC
Freeride.............................. **4** DH

Tweed - Innerleithen

Traquair XC Trail................ **4** XC
Make or Break..................... **2** DH
Red Bull............................. **3** DH
The Cresta Run................... **4** DH
The Matador....................... **5** DH

Ae

The Ae Line......................... **3** XC
Ae DH................................. **4** DH

Kirroughtree

Bargaly Wood..................... **1** XC
Larg Hill............................. **2** XC
The Twister......................... **3** XC
Black Craigs....................... **4** XC
Skills Area.......................... **4** XC

Mabie

Kona Dark Side................... **5** XC
Endura Phoenix Trail........... **3** XC
Woodhead Trail.................. **2** XC
Lochbank Trail.................... **2** XC
Big Views Trail................... **1** XC

Newcastleton

Skills Trail........................... **1** XC
The Caddrouns................... **2** XC
The Linns........................... **2** XC
Red Trail............................. **3** XC
Black Ridge........................ **4** XC

Glentrool

Big Country Trail................ **2** XC

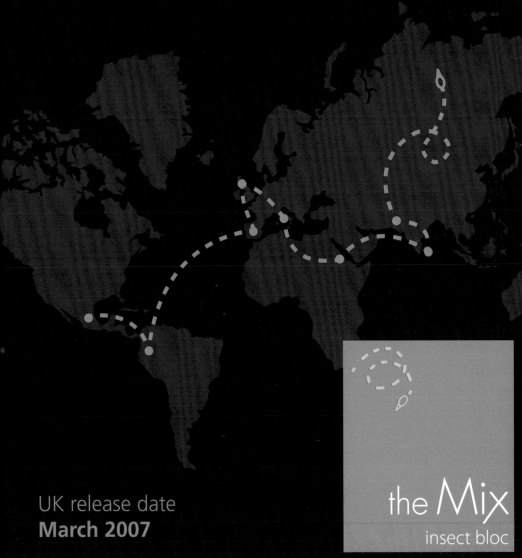

take yourself off the menu!

A unique natural formula developed
over 12 years worldwide to deliver
the ultimate insect repellent.

UK release date
March 2007

Visit insectsolutions.co.uk
for the full story

the Mix
insect bloc

Protection from
all biting insects

Outdoor Access in Scotland

The Land Reform (Scotland) Act came into force in February 2005, bringing with it one of the most progressive pieces of legislation in the world for outdoor recreation. But what does it mean for your average mountain biker? Basically, you have a right of access over most land in Scotland and this right applies equally to mountain bikers, ramblers, horse riders and anyone else not using a motor to propel themselves around, with none of the arbitrary distinction between 'footpaths' and 'bridleways' like there is south of the border in England and Wales.

Although the law in Scotland now gives mountain bikers some actual rights for the first time, it's worth taking a look at some of the detail. There's a right of access to 'most land', meaning there are some areas which are exempt; people's gardens, school grounds, farmyards, quarries, and fields of crops. There's another exclusion that covers 'land developed and in use for recreation', which means places like sports pitches and bowling greens. All common sense really, but now it's enshrined in law.

The buzz word in Scottish Access is RESPONSIBILITY. These new access rights only apply if you act responsibly. This might sound like a terribly grown-up approach to going for a bike ride, but it's a sound principle. It means you have to think about where you're going riding and what impact that might have on the land and other countryside users and then act accordingly. If there's been a heavy rainfall (not unusual in Scotland) then it's worth considering whether the trail you planned to ride might have turned into a bog which you'll carve a big rut in. Likewise, on a sunny day in the middle of July you might not want to go riding a trail that's promoted as a family walk, in both cases, if you did, legally you would be seen to be failing to act responsibly.

Most of this is common sense again - what would be considered irresponsible isn't the type of riding that most of us would want to do anyway – dragging your bike through a bog just isn't any fun. But this is an important point, as if mountain bikers are seen to cause erosion on certain routes, this could be used as justification for excluding riders from trails on the basis that they are 'not acting responsibly' and therefore do not have a right of access.

The guide to what is considered 'responsible' is meant to be covered in the Scottish Outdoor Access Code. In terms of cycling this says that riding on 'hard surfaces, such as wide paths and tracks', is not a problem.

When it comes to "peachy singletrack" (our term, not theirs), it says that cycling can cause problems for other users, and when this occurs you should dismount and walk until the path becomes suitable again.

Of course, you should always be considerate of other trail users and also of livestock. During lambing season

(March – June) you should be especially careful around sheep, or avoid them altogether. Also be aware that Scotland has a hunting season when people shoot deer and grouse. The grouse-shooting season is the main one to consider in southern Scotland and runs from 12th August – 10th December. To avoid being shot, make sure you check things out before heading to the hills. The local tourist office should be able to put you in touch with the local estates.

For the first time people have a clearly defined right of access in Scotland, it's not perfect, but it is very good. Now, go for a ride – it's virtually

your legal duty!

More info:

www.outdooraccess-scotland.com

The Access code.

www.scotways.com

Information on Rights of Way in Scotland. ROW in Scotland are not shown on the OS maps

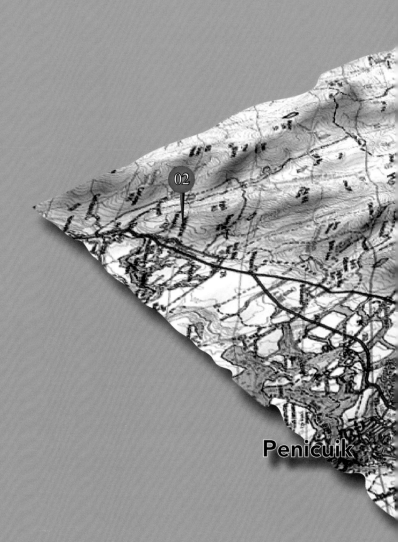

02

Penicuik

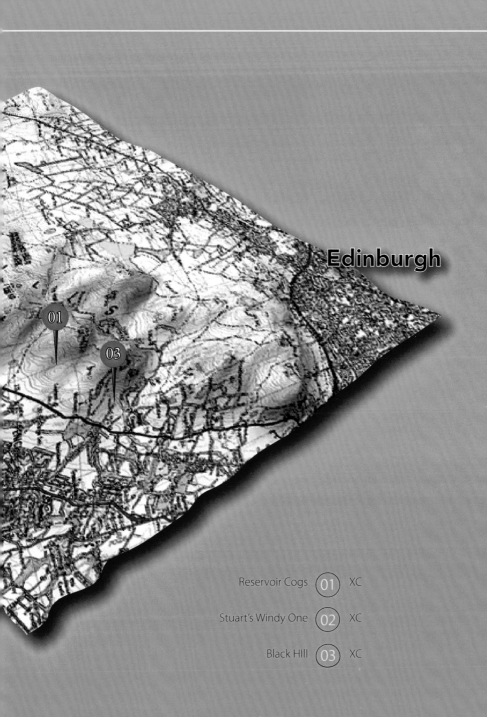

Edinburgh

Reservoir Cogs (01) XC

Stuart's Windy One (02) XC

Black HIll (03) XC

Introduction

Sitting above Edinburgh and running south west down towards Lanark, the Pentlands are a compact range of hills bordered by the A70 to the North and the A702 to the south.

The North-East Pentlands are easily accessible from Edinburgh. Princess Street is about a half hour ride from the hills here – you'll be hard pushed to find another capital city with this sort of playground right on the doorstep. Not surprisingly, this is a popular spot for local ramblers, dog walkers and mountain bikers, but if you're used to the hustle and bustle of more popular mountain regions you'll find the Pentlands pleasantly quiet and friendly. In contrast to the accessibility of the northern Pentlands, the southern Pentland Hills are much more off the beaten track and it's easy to feel quite remote in places.

There are tracks all over the place, making the Pentlands a place you could spend years exploring, we've just put together a taster of what's out there. The rides included here are often short and sharp, but the quality of the riding is beyond dispute, and it's easy enough to piece together a big day out in the hills by joining a couple of routes together.

Bear in mind that much of this land is grazed by sheep, so watch out for that during lambing season (March – June). Also, some of the routes here are 'summer only', as some of the Pentland tracks, such as Black Hill don't hold up too well in the wet.

Getting there

The Pentlands are located south-west of Edinburgh the Pentlands and are nestled in between the A70 and the A702.

From the Edinburgh & North

From the Edinburgh ring road, take the A70 towards Lanark as far as Balerno, then head for Harlaw reservoir or Red Moss wildlife Reserve.

Alternatively, head down the A702, towards Biggar and stop off at Flotterstone or Carlops

From the South

Leave the M74 at Junction 13 and take the A702 for Edinburgh. When you get to West Linton you're in the Pentlands.

Bike shops

Edinburgh has plenty of bike shops, here's a selection.

Edinburgh Bicycle Co-op on Alvanley Terrace, just off (Priness Street) EH9 1DU, in the heart of the city

www.edinburgh-bicycle.co.uk

Alpinebikes is also in Edinburgh at 48 Hamilton Place, EH3 5AX

www.alpinebikes.com

Bike Chain, 30 Rodney St, 0131 557 2801

www.thebikechain.co.uk

Locally there is Motavation in Penicuik tel 01968 673127, in the main it does car accessories but also carries some bike spares.

Eat, drink and sleep

We could write a book on where to eat and drink in Edinburgh, but we're not going to. Let's just say there are bars, take-away, chi-chi delicatessens, youth hostels, hotels and everything in between.

Closer to the hills there's less to choose from, but fortunately the standards seem pretty high. The Flotterstone Inn, on the A702, 3 miles beyond the ring road, does homemade burgers and Timothy Taylors Landlord.

The Allan Ramsay Hotel in Carlops is open all day and does good coffee, not to mention Deuchars IPA and Weise Bier fans will enjoy the draught Erdinger.

Useful contacts

www.edinburghguide.com
Where to stay, where to eat, what to do .

www.visitscotland.com
Comprehensive information on the area.

www.bikeknowledge.com
Bike Knowledge run courses and guiding based out of Edinburgh.

Summary

You'll soon realise why this is called Reservoir Cogs. On route you manage to visit six of the Pentlands finest watering holes, though not the alcoholic sort.

If you choose to do the ride in the evening or as an early morning run, then bar the odd curlew, buzzard and lark you'll likely have the trail to yourself.

Considering you're just a hair's breadth away from Edinburgh out here, the landscape and ambience of the Pentland Hills still manages to remain remote and uncompromised.

Flotterstone

Classic

2 with short sections of 3

24 km

675 m

2 - 3 hrs

OS Explorer 344

Getting There

There are a number of potential start points for this ride. Starting at Flotterstone, just South of Edinburgh means you save the best descent till last with a superb ride down the narrow Green Cleugh Glen polished off with a blast down the reservoir road back to the Visitor Centre. Alternatively shorten the ride slightly by doing the loop from a start point in the north, such as Bonaly or Harlaw Ranger Centre.

Start Point

Start at Car Park at the Ranger Centre just behind the Flotterstone Inn off the A702 which is just north of Penicuik and 3 miles south of the A720 Edinburgh ring road. From the Ranger Centre, ride up the Great Glen road towards Glencorse Lake. After riding alongside the reservoir for a short time, go over the inconspicuous Kirk Bridge and just after this is a large gate on the right with signs pointing you over to Bonaly.

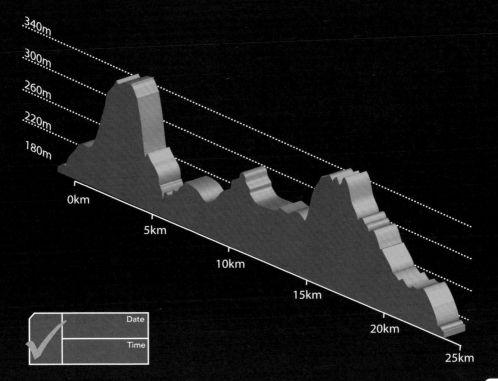

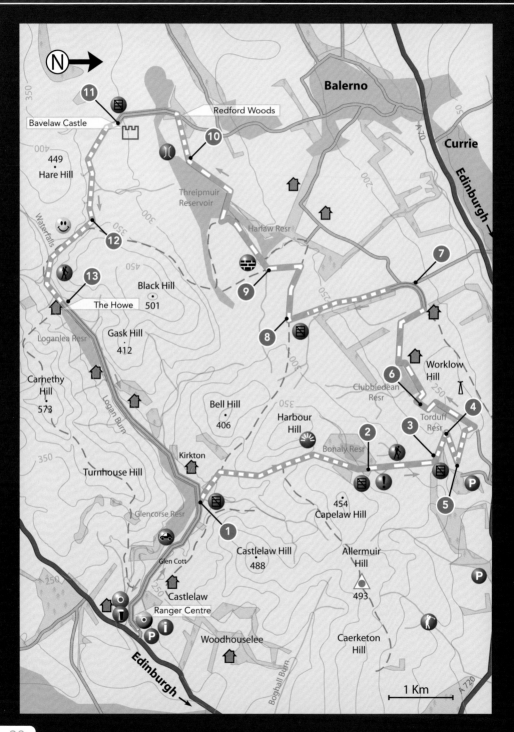

Route Description

1 Gate / Sign

Go through the gate and up the wide stony track alongside the small forest. As the hill starts to ease off, you come to a fork in the track. Take the right fork up and onto the open moorland. Go through a gate where the hill levels off and then continue pleasantly along the narrow rutted singletrack to arrive at the top of the forest at Bonaly Reservoir.

Go rightwards alongside the forest until you see a large gate into the forest and a wide track heading down towards Edinburgh in the distance.

2 Gate / Forest

Head straight down the wide track to another gate. With its small drainage ramps and big cobbles this can be a lot of fun, but watch your speed and watch out for overenthusiastic dogs!

After the gate the loosely surfaced track is even faster, be very aware of other users. This is a really fast section of trail. Don't expect to be able to stop in a hurry! With the loose surface you'll be surfing sideways before you know it.

The descent into Bonaly is very popular with dog walkers and ramblers and is well known as an accident black spot – so resist the urge to give gravity a run for its money and keep the speed well under control.

3 Gate / Woods

Go through the gate leading into the woods and take the small dirt path to the left. Roots and rocks make this gently contouring path entertaining, and early on a short section of steps will need ascending.

At the corner of the woods bear right following the path downwards to take the fall line for more twisting, rooty riding.

4 Torduff Hill

As you come out of the trees you are faced with the path up Torduff Hill. Turn right in the dip before the hill, and go down the grassy path to where the trail narrows to singletrack through gorse bushes and the odd muddy patch. Cross a path at a grassy clearing and continue until you meet the main trail crossing your path.

5 Main path

Turn left, going uphill briefly to come to a narrow brown ribbon of singletrack contouring around Torduff Hill. Follow this to be dropped off at the Torduff reservoir gate.

Go through the gate, cross the dam wall and turn right to continue riding alongside the reservoir.

6 Bend in road

At the end of the reservoir, stay on the tarmac to go steeply up to the next reservoir. Go along the north side of this one and stay on the track as far as the farm at Middle Kinleith.

Turn left on the road and continue 500 metres to a road junction. At the road junction go up the long straight dirt track on your left.

7 Secret singletrack

As you ride alongside the woods look to your left and you will see a small worn path weaving its way through the woods parallel to the track. Take your pick: track or singletrack, they both go to the same place.

At the end of the woods, go through a gate and continue 300 m in the same direction to the brow of the hill and a junction in the track.

8 Track junction

Turn right and head down towards Harlaw reservoir. Shortly after a gate, you come to a track junction in the middle of a flat field, take the left fork. Carry on along the track to where the track runs alongside trees and an old stone wall. Before the next gate, go over the wall at an old stone steps stile.

9 Stone Stile

On the other side of the wall go left taking the wide path around Threipmuir reservoir. Go over the weir to cross the reservoir and turn left to follow the flat path alongside the water. Ignore the first bridge on your left (private) and continue to Redford Woods.

10 Redford Woods

At a bend in the track, the path goes straight on into the woods. Take this for some more secret singletrack. Exit this onto a minor road and turn left to go over the Redford Bridge.

On the other side of the bridge, pump your way up the steep tarmac to a T junction at the top. Go left at the junction and then first right. Pass the entrance to Bavelaw Castle and continue a short distance up the gravel track to a gate leading out onto the moor.

11 Bavelaw Castle / Gate

Take the wide grassy trail leftwards to a slight rise. Over the rise the trail narrows and turns into a smooth snaking piece of singletrack, which almost looks as if it has been purpose built for us. Relax in the saddle, let it flow, and enjoy yourself all the way.

12 Green Cleugh Descent

At a gate the hills suddenly close in, creating a narrow glen with a rutted path running down the middle of it. This is the final descent and one to truly savour. There is nothing too technical and a choice of lines allows you choose the difficulty and then let gravity do the work. Ride, grinning, to the lake.

13 The Howe

At the bottom the path widens out into a multitude of lines. Take the track heading to the left hand side of the reservoir and blast on down the Glen road and back to the Ranger Centre.

Summary

'Stu's Windy One' takes you from one side of the Pentlands to the other and then back again, and while the highest elevation on the route is a relatively modest at 480m, you'll feel as if you've done your fair share of climbing by the end. The ride has a bit of everything, from farm tracks to heather moorland singletrack, together with some challenging climbs and joyous descents.

Hard to believe that you're never more than 10 miles from Edinburgh city centre, but don't underestimate this terrain, it's pretty exposed in places and once you set off there are no refreshment stops and no real escape options until you get back to Carlops. So make sure you go prepared.

Carlops	
Classic	
Hard	3
25 km	
580 m	
2 - 3 hrs	
OS Explorer 344	

Getting there

Carlops is on the A702, south west of Penicuik and
9 miles south West from the Edinburgh ring Road.
There's a car park by 'Witch's Rock', opposite the
church.

Start

From the car park you can see the tarmac track on
the other side of the main road, signposted for
'Buteland by the Borestane'. Follow the track uphill, ignoring the left turn to Carlophill Farm,
and continue to Fairliehope Farm.

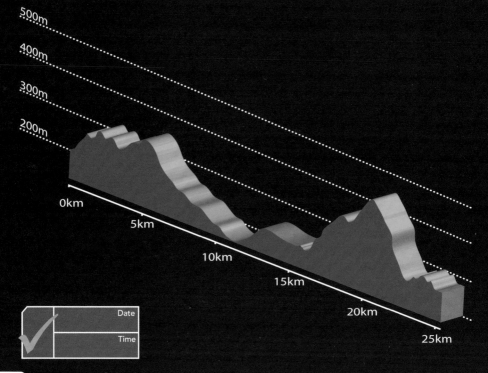

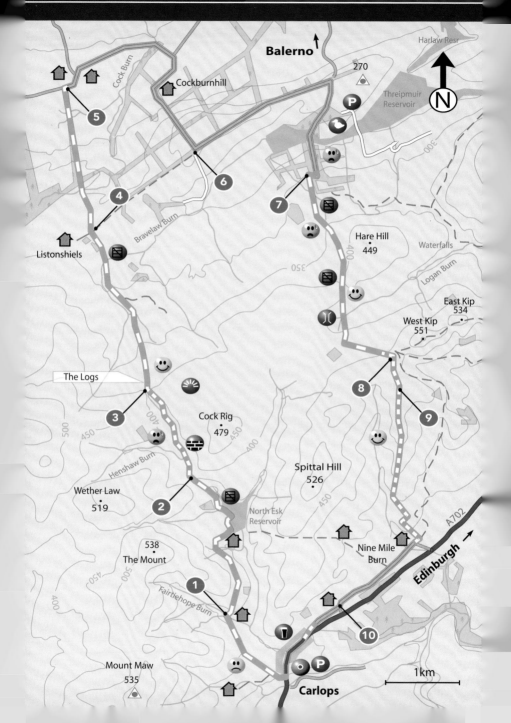

Harlaw Resr

Balerno

270

Threipmuir
Reservoir

N

Cockburnhill

P

300

6

4

400

Hare Hill
449

Waterfalls

Listonshiels

Bravelaw Burn

350

Logan Burn

7

East Kip
534

West Kip
551

The Logs

Cock Rig
479

450
400

500

3

8

9

Spittal Hill
526

Henshaw Burn

Wether Law
519

450
400

2

North Esk
Reservoir

A702

Nine Mile
Burn

538
The Mount

1

Fairliehope Burn

Edinburgh

400

450

500

Mount Maw
535

10

1km

Carlops

P

Route Description

 Fairliehope

The track turns left at the farm buildings, still climbing, but it soon levels out as North Esk Reservoir comes into view straight ahead. Keep on the obvious wide stone track as it leads you down to the reservoir.

The track ends at a house by the reservoir, follow the Right of Way signs to the left through the gate and follow the grassy doubletrack along the side of the reservoir, you'll soon find yourself climbing steadily up into the hills again, following the signposts for 'Buteland', up through the narrow gully between Cock Rig and Whether Law.

 Skinny Bridges

Go through the gate and follow the path as it weaves through the bog grass, across a couple of skinny wooden bridges and over the burn. Immediately afterwards you've got a short, steep climb on what looks like a sheep track – own the climb!

Or get off and push if you prefer. Just around the corner the lungs can recover briefly as the trail descends on a gorgeous ribbon of singletrack, before pointing upwards again to cross over a wall.

Classic moorland riding now. Go straight on up through the heather, the track is obvious, but the tightness of the trail along with a few boulders and occasional boggy section makes for a sporting climb up to the Borestane.

3 The Top /Borestane

Cross over the style and enjoy the view across Edinburgh and the Solway Firth. The signpost to 'Buteland' shows you the way straight on down through the heather. You quickly join a doubletrack, which is easy to spot because its made of logs. Turn right, riding over the logs and on down the hill. Don't ride around them, this only adds to the erosion problems here.

After the all the logs you join a stony section of doubletrack. Ignore the grassy track that forks right, keep left and enjoy the descent. After 1km you go through a gate and continue straight on with woodland on your left.

 Gate / Track junction

After the gate you meet a surfaced track. Continue straight on, following the sign for 'Balerno by Buteland'. After 700m you cross a cattlegrid. The track is now rough tarmac and continues dead straight for about 1.5km until you meet the road.

5 Minor Road

Turn right at the road. Ignore the huge house in front of you, you can't afford it. Bear right at the triangle of roads and at the next junction turn right and pass under the pylons.

After Cockburnhill Farm there's a steady climb with optional rooty singletrack amongst the trees to the left.

 T Junction

Go left along a very straight road. [(if you were deranged enough to take the "tussock shortcut" earlier you should come out here, in which case go straight on when you hit the road)]. At the next junction turn right towards Red Moss Wildlife Reserve.

When you hit the reserve bear right following the sign post for '9 Mile Burn and Glencourse'. You cross a Stoney Bridge which bears you across Threipmuir Reservoir and you can now see 'Exponential Hill' rearing up in front of you. Enjoy it! At the top of the hill turn right and after 50m take a left, at the signpost for '9 Mile Burn'.

7 'Nine Mile Burn' signpost

If the weather's a bit blustery this is a good place to stop, have a rest and a bite to eat amongst the trees - this is your last chance of any cover. Go through the gate and you're back onto open moorland with a conifer plantation on your left which you soon leave behind as you spin on up the hill. The grassy track climbs steadily upwards with a dry stone wall to the left then you get a bit of a breather as you drop down to a stone bridge.

Let's climb again! You can see the line of the trail bearing right at first then contouring left up to a shoulder below the very steep sides of West Kip.

8 Stile

Cross over the fence to your right following sign for '9 Mile Burn'. There's a vague singletrack trail heading up the hill which soon bisects another track and then becomes wider and more obvious as it continues upwards. Below and on your left is woodland which you will lose sight of as you keep climbing. When

you reach a fork in the track, bear right.

9 Top of Cap Law

Fun time. Remember all that climbing? Well, here's the reward: a blast down the grassy south ridge of Cap Law all the way down to 9 Mile Burn. Check out the Font Stone on the way and soak up the heritage, then point your bike downhill and get back to business. You might notice some wind around here too, this is quite normal.

As you get lower down there are two stiles to cross. After crossing the second one go left following the fence line down the hill towards the main road. When you hit the stone wall, go right following another sign post for '9 Mile Burn', then left over a stile and down again along the side of a field. Turn right at the bottom and head for the cottages, through the gate and continue straight on up the tarmac road heading back to Carlops.

10 Wanton Wa's

Take the right turn at Wanton Wa's cottage instead of going down to the main road. Head on up until the track switches back to the right, at which point carry straight on down the grassy track. This section of track offers a few tasty bits. Careful with the steps at the end. If you get them wrong you'll be sprawled across the A702 – not the grand finale you really want. You can see Carlops now. Turn right on the main road and back to the Car park.

Summary

This route is a little gem. The descent down the side of Black Hill makes a reasonable claim to be the best bit of trail in the Pentlands – no idle boast. Maybe it is so revered because it's so elusive. It's definitely a fair weather ride, the soft peat of Black Hill is unrideable unless you're kicking up dust! To attempt to ride this in the winter or after summer rains would ruin the trail and ruin your ride, so be sensitive.

There is a foul weather version of this ride which goes onto Bavelaw Castle and around the other side of Threipmuir reservoir and makes a fine ride in itself.

The 600m of ascent feels like a lot more due to some tough climbs. If you can ride them all you should consider yourself a bike-god!

Camoflauge Hill is often used by the local barracks for exercises, don't be alarmed if you see the undergrowth

Flotterstone	
Expert	
Hard	3
23 km	
600 m	
2 - 3 hrs	
OS Explorer 344	

moving – it'sprobably just some blokes with guns. On one night ride a local mountain biker took a fall here and landed on one of these squadies who up until then was doing an excellent job of hiding from the enemy. True story!

And once you're finished you can treat yourself to a pint of Landlord and a homemade burger at the Flotterstone Inn – you'll have well and truly earned it!

Getting there

Start at Car Park at the Ranger Centre just behind the Flotterstone Inn, off the A702 just north of Penicuik, 3 Miles south of the A720 Edinburgh ring road.

Start

Take the tarmac road that heads off past the Ranger Centre and within a few minutes Glencourse Reservoir will come into view. Stay on the road past Glencourse and up to Loganlea reservoir, at the end of which the road becomes a track which after 50m takes a left turn to cross Loganlea Burn.

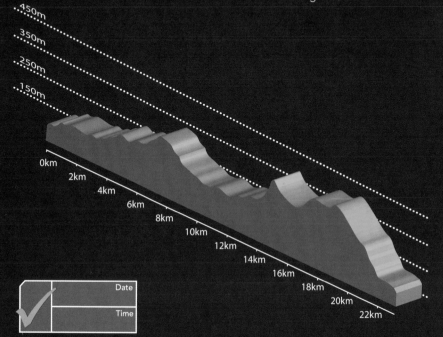

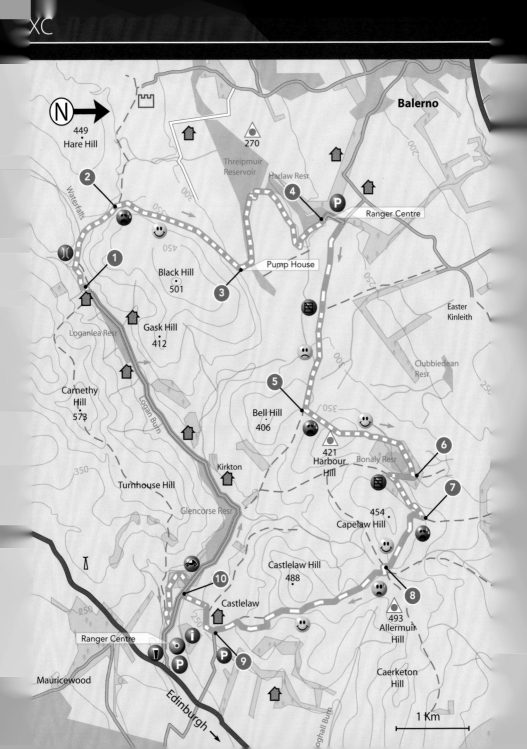

XC Route Description

1 Logan Burn Crossing

After crossing Logan Burn the track turns immediately right following the sign for Balerno taking you into a narrow gully.

A lovely bit of trail criss-crosses the burn on grassy and rocky bits of singletrack. As the glen gets narrower the trail becomes slightly wider, but still fun. Stay in the gully, ignoring the brutal climb that cuts left.

2 Sheep track climb

A stony track cuts sharply up to your right, cutting through the heather – a tricky climb that tests your strength and balance.

As the track levels off you meet a wall, and Threipmuir Reservoir comes into view. The wall on your left will guide you to the reservoir, the path is obvious though and superbly swoopy. It seems like the mix of peat, heather and boulders have been arranged perfectly for our enjoyment. There's a sharp left as you approach the reservoir and then drop down to the pumping house. You should now be feeling very happy by now.

3 Pumping house

Cross the stile and the reservoir then go left following the sign for 'Threipmuir Car Park'.

Follow the trail along the north side of the reservoir which takes you into a tunnel of trees. When you emerge from the trees, drop down onto a wide stone path and go left and immediately right, taking another wide path through a gap in the wall.

If you have the time to explore there's some fun singletrack in the trees at the south end of Harlaw Reservoir.

This area is very popular with dog walkers and families so be aware and be considerate. You're now skirting around Harlaw reservoir which should be visible through the trees on your left and will eventually arrive at Harlaw Ranger Centre.

4 Harlaw Ranger Centre

Go through the gate and you have a short section of tarmac which immediately bends right. After 150m you turn right opposite the car park and take the wide track across the field. After 200m take the left fork signposted for 'Glencourse' on the surfaced track leading you back into the hills.

At the gate ignore the track to the left for Currie and continue straight on, following the stone wall on your right. It's a nice climb to the top of the pass with a few shallow steps on the way.

5 Top of the Pass

Go through the gate, Glencourse Reservoir is straight ahead down below you, so this is an obvious bail out point if you're flagging a bit. The route now turns left straight up to the top of Harbour Hill. Keep your front wheel grounded and try and ride to the top!

You'll know when you hit the top because of the superb views out across Edinburgh and the Solway Firth. Look down and you'll also see Bonaly Reservoir ahead, surrounded by conifers. You're heading for the left side of this reservoir, so look for the singletrack breaking left to the fence as soon as you start going downhill.

There's a junction of collapsed walls where you cross the fence and a grassy path leads downhill. You're heading for the trees on your right, so ignore any paths that split left. As you get lower down the slope the path widens and becomes quite obvious. You hug the woodland until you hit a big wide dirt track.

6 Puke Hill

Turn right, go through the gate and head uphill. After another 300m you reach a gate where you turn left, following the sign for 'Allermuir'. Bear right at the fork – and continue the steady climb, heading straight for a steep grass slope, but at the bottom of this you turn sharp left and follow a sheep track that contours up around the shoulder of a hillock. You soon come to a wide dirt track where you turn sharp right.

7 Camoflauge Hill

Tough climb this next bit, if you can ride it you should consider turning pro. The track soon levels out though before contouring around the north-east shoulder of Capelaw Hill and another pleasant grass track descent brings you down to a gate.

From the top you've got a very quick descent, for a bit of variety you can head left on the wide grassy track then bear right in the direction of Penicuik and the masts over at Marchwell. You soon rejoin the stony track you were on previously and continue down to a gate.

9 Castlelaw

Go straight across here to the small gate to the left of the farmhouse, signposted for 'Glencourse' - this leads onto a rooty singletrack that circumvents the farm. When you join the doubletrack on the other side of the farm head back towards the hills to another gate, after which turn left down the hill, signposted to Flotterstone.

This track snakes downwards with a few stone water bars to add some sport - very popular with walkers so WATCH YOUR SPEED!

10 Back at the road

At the road you can turn left for the car park, but for one final treat turn right and head up the road 100m, take a left through the wall signposted for 'Flotterstone by Old Filterbeds'. Head down through the trees then follow the burn back to the road. When you hit the road you should be able to see the car park ahead. Turn right and you'll be there in 60 secs.

More rides in the Pentlands

If you live in Edinburgh you'll no doubt spend a lot of time in this bunch of hills. Just a stone's throw from the city and yet full of quite little frequented trails. It's the sort of place where every time you go out on one ride, you spot the potential for a new line and before you know it you are putting together your own trail versions all over the place.

Don't forget though if you are making up your own variations, that the ground here is very sensitive to damage especially during the rainy season. The Pentland Hills Regional Park offers advice on this, and this can be found in the on-line publications at www.edinburgh.gov.uk/phrp. There are also advisory markers to be found in the hills indicating the paths suitability for cycling.

As well as the rides detailed in the route descriptions for this section, here are a few others to go and sample.

Water of Leith
Family 12km Ascent 130m

There are loads of easy paths with level surfaces around the water Leith and the reservoir network south of Edinburgh.

A marked cycle route follows the Water of Leith from Balerno into Edinburgh. You can follow it all the way to the Castle if you want. A quiet family ride option is to start in Balerno, go along to Currie. Turn right here to Wester Kinleith and continue up the track on to the open hills. At the first T junction in the track head right to go down to Harlaw reservoir along the side of Thriepmuir Reservoir and back down the minor road to Balerno.

Mendick Hill Circuit
Classic / Blast 26.5km Ascent 400m

Taking in old roman roads, gentle wide tracks, expansive moorland, and restrained descents, the Mendick Circuit offers a peaceful day out in the south of the hills.

Start in Carlops on the A702, head along the pavement west for a short time to then cross the road and follow signs to old roman road to West Linton. Here go past the golf course towards Slipperfields and the reservoir. Follow the track up on to the hill, and then the only piece of navigational difficulty on the ride, a faint path just before you descend to the Medwin River, takes you to a stand of trees and a track leading left out of the trees. Follow the track to Ferniehaugh Farm. Go through the farmyard and turn right to Garvald. At Garvald follow the road to Mon, taking the track back to West Linton to retrace your steps back to Carlops.

You can shorten this ride by starting and finishing in West Linton, or if you want to keep it really simple just go from Carlops to West Linton and back to give you an easy family friendly ride.

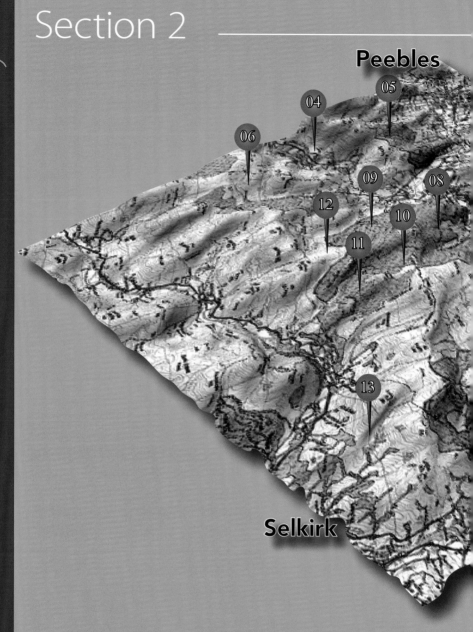

The Tweed Valley

Peebles

Selkirk

04
05
06
08
09
10
11
12
13

07

Innerleithen

Introduction

You'd be forgiven for believing that the Tweed Valley consists of just one forest, Glentress, with a spectacular array of mountain biking trails. In truth, you'll find quality trails all along the stretch of the River Tweed as it runs 30km from Lyne Water near Peebles to Ettrick Water near Selkirk. Amongst these rolling hills lie over 300km of cracking trails. You could spend a week in the valley and not ride the same trail twice.

Glentress is indeed the jewel in the crown of the Tweed Valley, and arguably British mountain biking. Here you'll find every type of trail for every type of mountain biker, with more trails being built by the day. There is plenty of swooping singletrack on the way-marked 7stanes runs, hidden singletrack courtesy of the trail fairies volunteer group and the Freeride Park shows the latest face of the Tweed Valley courtesy of some heavy machinery.

Escape from the trail centres and there are plenty of thrills to be found amongst the old drove roads and riverside paths of the valley. There are quick blasts up and down the side of the valley, classic rides circumnavigating the towns and epic all-day rides linking the forests over ancient drove roads. Not to mention the extreme challenges of the Project Downhill trails at Innerleithen.

There is a real buzz about the Tweed Valley. Thanks to some forward thinking local enthusiasts and Forestry Commission Scotland staff, the area has transformed itself into a 'No 1' world-class mountain biking destination. You just have to stand on Peebles High Street for 5 minutes and see how many cars drive through with bikes on the back. The local community is really embracing the movement and you'll find plenty of apres-trail hospitality to match the riding experience. Spend a while and take it all in.

Getting there

The Tweed Valley lies 20 miles south of Edinburgh in the Scottish Borders. There are no train lines into the Borders, but Edinburgh is served by a train station, airport and ferry terminal. All of the main budget and regular airlines fly into Edinburgh and Glasgow. Superfast ferries link Rosyth, north of Edinburgh with Zeebrugge on the continent. The no.62 bus goes from Edinburgh through the borders towns.

Driving from the south - you have a couple of options. Form the north-east of England you can jump off the A1 at Newcastle and take the A696 and A68 into the heart of the Borders. From the north-west the M6 an M74 take you across the border and you take the A701 from Moffat towards Peebles or the A708 towards Selkirk.

From the north - Peebles is an hours' drive south from Edinburgh on the A703 or an hour and a half southwest of Glasgow on the A72.

Local services

Whether you are using Peebles, Innerleithen or Selkirk as a base, there are places to eat, drink and get stocked up on supplies and you'll be able to fill up on petrol in Peebles and Selkirk. Each town has a small supermarket with Peebles being the best bet for stocking up for a week. They also have delicatessens, bakers and sweet shops!

The three main towns have pubs which serve good bar food. In Peebles, you can find good pub grub in The Crown, the Neidpath and County Inns. In addition to this, The Tontine and Green Tree hotels do pub grub and a la carte food. There is also the usual mix of Italian, Indian and Asian restaurants. In Innerleithen The Traquair Arms, close to Project Downhill, does good food and drink.

Accommodation

The Tweed Valley has come along in leaps and bounds with tailoring accommodation to mountain bikers' needs. You'll find much accommodation with secure bike stores, drying rooms, kit washing facilities and even bike workstands. There are B&Bs and hotels nestled next to the trail centres and bunkhouses ideally located in the hills for some of the classic rides in this section.

Glentress has the aptly named Glentress Hotel, on its doorstep which caters for mountain bikers and with new owners has introduced a tasty menu to boot. In Peebles itself, there are plenty of Inns, B&Bs and Hotels, including the Tontine Hotel, in the centre of town and out of town the Winkston farmhouse B&B is popular with mountain bikers and also has self catering cottages for a longer stay.

In Innerleithen the bike lodge, caters for every mountain bikers' whim and offers self catering accommodation for weekends and longer breaks. The Traquair Arms, .co.uk is a friendly Inn which also offers self catering accommodation.

Bike shops

The Tweed Valley has four main bike shops

spread along the river. In Peebles, the community based shop is Border Bike Sport, (01721 723423) in Pennels close off the high street. This friendly shop deals with sales, repairs and supplies. Along in Glentress Forest itself is the Hub bike shop and café (01721 721736). The Hub offers a range of services to mountain bikers including sales, repairs, tuition, uplift and world-class cake. They also run an uplift service for the downhill trails at Innerleithen.

In Innerleithen there is another Pro Bikesport shop on the high street. Responsible for a lot of trail building in their spare time, the guys in the shop can fix your bike or hire you an alternative. Along at Galashiels, Tony runs The Rush bike shop (01896 757674) on Market Street. This is the closest shop to Selkirk, which does not have a bike shop of its own, and offers sales, repairs and hire bikes.

Local guides and MTB operators

There are plenty of operators offering guided tours, holidays and coaching in the area and in the end it comes down to personal preference as to whom you go with.

MB7 run by Iain Withers, our very own co-writer, runs a very excellent guiding and skills training programme and also arranges tailor made holidays to suit individual needs. Iain also recommends the Hub for advanced training and often works with Macs Adventure,

Useful contacts

www.syha.org.uk

www.scot-borders.co.uk

www.visittweeddale.com

www.7stanes.gov.uk

www.mb7.com

www.macsadventure.com.

www.therush.uk.com

www.thehubintheforest.co.uk

www.probikesport.com

www.glentress.org.uk

www.tontinehotel.com

www.traquair-arms-hotel

www.thebikelodge.co.uk

Gypsy's Descent

Glentress & Peebles

Summary

Gypsy's Descent gets your heart pumping quickly with a long gradual climb before keeping it beating hard with an exhilarating descent. For a quick fix, you take in what is widely regarded as the finest descent in the hills around Peebles. What's more, it's been there for centuries and hardly ever gets ridden. The route forms the northern end of the 'Gypsy Glen' drover's road from St Mary's Loch to Peebles.

Ride it fast and you'll be at the top in under an hour and down in half that time.

If you enjoy gaining height quickly without too much in the way of a challenge, the first half of this ride is just for you. Before you know it you're on to the undulating descent

Glentress	
Blast	
Hard	3
20 km	
600 m	
1 - 3 hrs	
Landranger 73	

The final section of the ride taking you into Peebles can be ridden at full steam, but you'll have to keep an eye out for walkers climbing the other way! This blast can leave a serious grin on your face.

Getting there

From Peebles follow signs for Innerleithen. After 2 miles, turn left into Glentress Forest before the Glentress Hotel. From Innerleithen, follow signs for Peebles. After 4 miles turn right into Glentress Forest after the Glentress Hotel.

Start Point

Hub car park, Glentress Forest

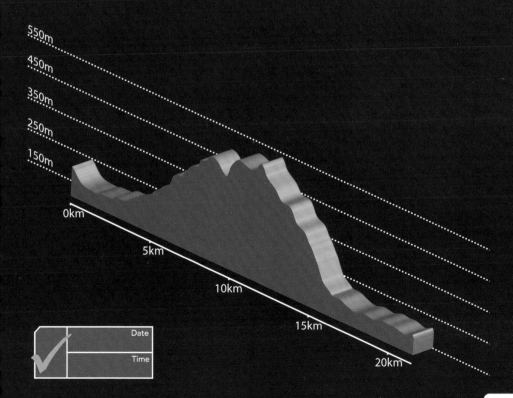

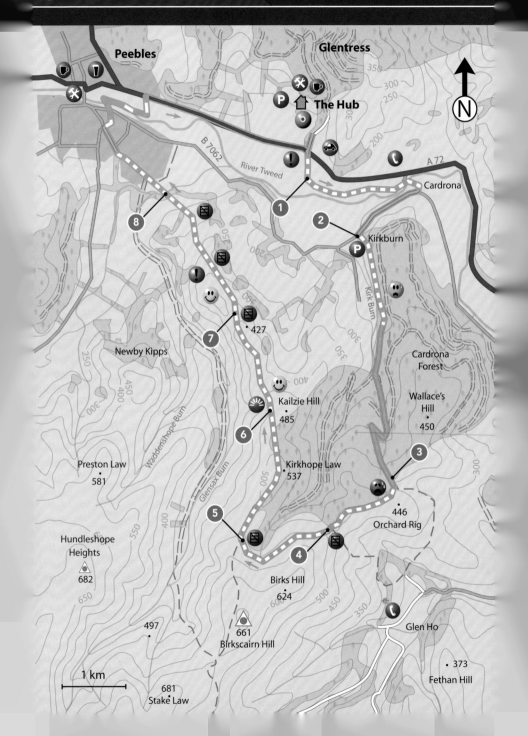

Peebles

Glentress

The Hub

B 7062

River Tweed

A 72

Cardrona

Kirkburn

Kirk Burn

Cardrona Forest

Newby Kipps

· 427

Wallace's Hill
· 450

Waddenshope Burn

Kailzie Hill
· 485

Preston Law
· 581

Glensax Burn

Kirkhope Law
· 537

· 446
Orchard Rig

Hundleshope Heights
△ 682

Birks Hill
· 624

· 497

△ 661
Birkscairn Hill

Glen Ho

· 373
Fethan Hill

1 km

681
Stake Law

N

Route Description

Hub Car Park

From the car park (or café more likely) ride back to the main road and cross over (with great care - cars can fly along this road). Take the path opposite the hotel leading away from the main road past the ruined tower on your left. Ignore the left turning in to the quarry and continue through the gate, veering left towards the river. Take the time to take in the meandering river.

1 Riverside Path

Follow the river downstream (left) along the old railway line until you reach the bridge over the river. Cross the bridge and follow the well surfaced path through the golf course towards the hillside to the south. As you near the hillside, cross the grass to the stream and cross the gate, climbing up to the road. Turn right and follow the road for 500m, before turning into the Cardrona Forest car park

2 Cardrona Forest

In the car park, turn left and cross the bridge at the start of the way-marked walks. Follow the group of way-markers up the climb onto the forest doubletrack.

Follow the doubletrack south as it climbs into the forest and continue for 3km ensuring not to take any right turns. After 3km the path hairpins right and then left, continue along this path for a further 1km until a left turn towards a clearing.

Take this left turn until you come out of the forest and continue to a gate. Do not worry if you miss this turning and find yourself at a dead-end turning circle. Simply follow a direct line ahead through the forest and you will reach the boundary trail.

3 Boundary Trail

You are now following the edge of the forest clockwise. At the southern edge of the forest, follow the steep singletrack climb around the boundary of the forest. This is very steep and you may find yourself walking. Continue around the boundary for 1.5km as the trail climbs and then steeply descends. At the end of the steep descent, on the edge of the forest, turn south through the gate.

4 Birks Hillside

Follow the trail contouring around the open hillside. This 1km climb is steep to start with but soon levels off. Make sure you don't turn left up the steep eroded climb to Birkscairn Hill, but continue to contour around the hill until the path surface improves considerably. There is a short descent to the edge of the forest, before the trail levels and meets the fence marking the ridge line.

5 The Ridge

Follow the ridge north alongside the forest as it undulates towards the top of Kailzie Hill. Riding the whole length of this ridge is a joy and there is a choice of lines with two or three different ruts to choose from. Inevitably, whichever rut you choose to descend will fill with rocks and you have to hop into another! To get the most out of riding the ridge, the trail is best ridden when it's been dry or when full of snow!

6 Kailzie Hill Descent

This is where the real fun begins - get your favourite speed-freak face on and let go of the brakes. It can be hard work switching between the ruts to keep your momentum and the ability to side-hop will definitely be well rewarded.

Looking ahead to see when your rut is going to fill up with rocks is a good idea and resist the temptation to ride on the heather – that's cheating! After just over 1km you'll go down a steep dip – keep your speed up – and up a short ride to a gate.

7 The Last Blast

There are two more gates to go through on the next section. This can kill your momentum, unless your buddies are holding them open for you. After the gate follow the fast grassy descent around the hill to the metal gate. After the gate continue the grassy descent through the next metal gate.

This is very fast and you will have to keep an eye out for walkers as you go . After the second gate, the trail narrows and turns into singletrack which descends to arrive at a river crossing at th bottom.

Go on – get wet!

8 Back to The Hub

Follow the trail up through the wooden stile and continue straight ahead to the road. Follow the road into Peebles for 1km until you pass the park on your right. Go down the steep steps into the park and follow the path to the main road and over the Tweed on the iron bridge.

Turn downstream and follow the path into the playing grounds. Follow the edge of the pitches north up to the main road. From here you can cross and climb into Glentress Forest via Jenny's Brae if you have time to spare. If not, follow the pavement on the south side of the road back to Glentress.

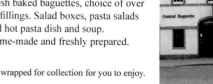

EDINBURGH **BICYCLE** COOPERATIVE

MASSIVE CHOICE

Probably the most complete range of bicycle equipment and cycle clothing you'll find under one roof.

THE BEST BICYCLES

From the best names in cycling – Specialized, Cannondale and Giant – plus Edinburgh Bicycle's own award-winning Revolution bikes.

GUARANTEED REPAIRS & SERVICES

A Service Menu to suit every need – anything from a puncture repair to a complete bicycle strip-down and rebuild. Our mechanics are sussed in suspension technology and delight in disc brake disassembly.

Tel: 0845 257 0808

Open 7 days a week.

ABERDEEN SHOP

458-464 George Street, Aberdeen AB25 3XH.

EDINBURGH SHOP

8 Alvanley Terrace, Whitehouse Loan, Edinburgh EH9 1DU.

LEEDS SHOP

140 Woodland Lane, Leeds LS7 4QG.

NEWCASTLE SHOP

5-7 Union Road, Byker, Newcastle-upon-Tyne NE6 1EH.

Cademuir Loop

Glentress & Peebles

Summary

The Cademuir loop out of Peebles gives a great feel for the history of the area together with providing a surprise or two along the way for the accomplished mountain biker. This half-day ride includes spectacular views of the Tweed Valley, and offers an insight into Tweeddale life both past and present. This is a ride to take the camera with you.

Riding straight out of the market town, you are rewarded by some surprisingly technical climbing and descending on easy-to-follow trails. The dominant feature of the ride is the Cademuir ridge, with a great descent through Iron Age hill forts.

This is a ride combining man-made switchbacks with timeless passes. For the time you spend on the bike, there are few rides that can offer more in the area. This is a great starting point for Tweed Valley off-piste riding.

Peebles

Classic

Moderate

22 km

650 m

2 - 3 hrs

Landranger 73

Getting there

Peebles is a small market town which has been thrown into the mountain biking limelight by the phenomenon that is Glentress Forest. It is 20 miles south of Edinburgh, at the intersection of the A703 and A72.

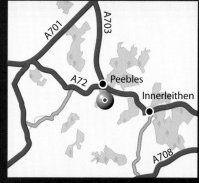

Start Point

The start point of the loop is Border Bike Sport, which is a friendly community bike shop in Pennels Close at the east end of the High Street. Here you will find all the spares and repairs you would need with plenty of bakers and sweety shops around to fuel up.

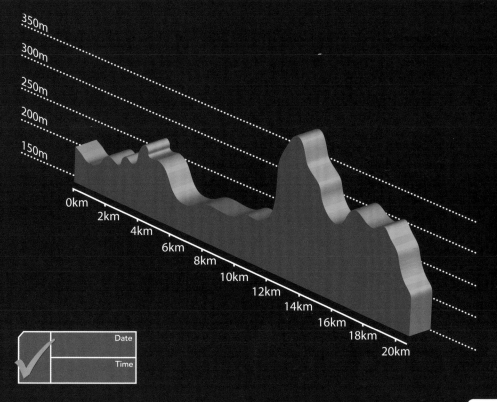

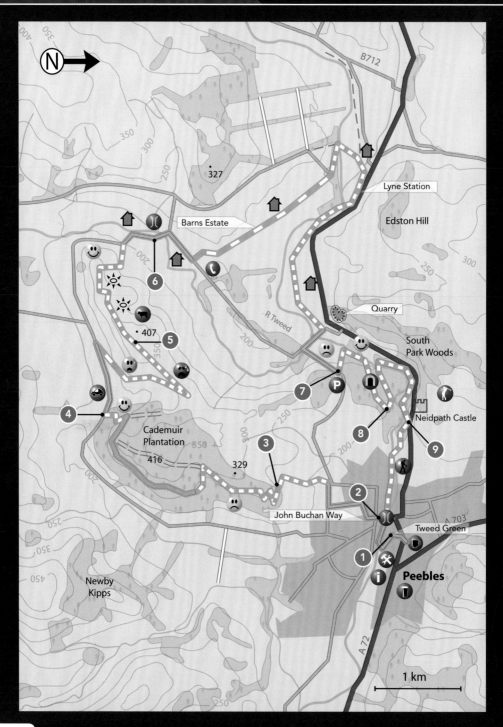

N

B712

Lyne Station

Edston Hill

327

Barns Estate

6

407

5

R Tweed

Quarry

South
Park Woods

7

P

Neidpath Castle

8

9

Cademuir
Plantation

416

329

4

3

John Buchan Way

2

Tweed Green

1

Peebles

Newby
Kipps

A 703

A 72

1 km

XC Route Description

1 Tweed Green

Exit from the bike shop vennel (translation for southerners: vennel = passageway) and turn left, followed by the very next left through the next vennel. Follow the road down to 'Tweed Green' and cross the Tweed over the iron footbridge.

Take the time to absorb your surroundings as the river flows through the town. Follow the footpath upstream to the road bridge and climb up onto the road.

2 John Buchan Way

Turn left on the bridge and right with care as the road forks. Turn immediately left and up the steep tarmac footpath. From here, follow the 'John Buchan Way' through Peebles to a black gate on the edge of a field signposted for Manor Valley.

From here you escape from Peebles and begin the real mountain biking. Follow the edge of the wall on your left to the gate. From here, turn left and aim for the metal gate signposted 'Tweed Trails' leading into Cademuir Forest.

3 Cademuir Forest

Shortly after the gate, turn right and follow the Tweed Trails waymarkers up a 'rude-awakening' singletrack climb. Follow 'Tantah's trail' (green waymarkers) up the singletrack climb and then onto a fast doubletrack descent to the forest track for your first adrenaline buzz. At the forest track, turn right and continue through the gate into the forest, following 'Tweed Trails' markers. After 1km take the left fork in

Take the multiple switchback descent down the singletrack on your left to the road.

4 Cademuir Climb

Throughout this section you can see your goal – the summit of the Cademuir ridge, looming above you. Turn right on the road and follow the tarmac for 1km until you go past a lone stand of pine trees on your right. Turn right onto singletrack and follow the climbing trail past the pine trees up to a wall on the edge of a field.

Follow the wall left for a further 1km until you reach a post with yellow marker. Turn sharp left and follow the double track up to the summit of Cademuir Hill.

Be prepared for a steep climb which is definitely in 'bike and hike' territory. As the doubletrack levels out into a saddle, ensure you turn left up onto the summit of Cademuir Hill.

5 Cademuir Ridge

Follow the ridge for 1.5km as it undulates from east to west. This is one of the highlights of the route and includes short rocky descents which spring up on you. Along the way, you pass ancient forts and settlements centuries old. It is easy to understand why there were forts up here when you peer down the imposing bankings of the ridge.

Follow the ridge along to its end for a final view before descending. Just before the final peak turn north on the vague doubletrack and descend past the sheep pen and down to the road.

Turn right on the road which passes cottages and follows Manor water downstream to a

6 Picnic Spot

After munchies, cross the Iron Bridge and turn right at the road junction. After 500m take a left along the track just after the red phone box to take you into Barns Estate. Follow the track straight to the end, taking the second left turn signposted for Tweed Cycleway. This is a singletrack trail which quickly reaches a bridge crossing the Tweed.

Follow signs for 'Tweed Walk' up the road until the old railway bridge. Climb up on to the railway path and follow the old railway line east for 2km. to the road. Turn right and cross over the Tweed once again.

Turn left at the first turning, over 'Old Manor Brig' and up the steep tarmac climb to the viewpoint at the edge of South Park Wood. Enjoy the view along the Tweed.

7 South Park Wood

Enter South Park Wood on the north side of the road and take the steep singletrack descent, following the line of the wall. As the Tweed comes into view, take the right fork onto a doubletrack climb.

When the trail reaches the old railway bridge, turn right and enter the tunnel. This is a disused (obviously!) railway tunnel which has the habit of spooking bikers. But no worries, the surface is good and riding with only one basic light is definitely recommended for an experience! After 500m you emerge back into daylight.

8 Technical Singletrack

Just after you emerge from the tunnel, cross a stream and turn immediately left down some steep steps. Turn left at the bottom and follow the riverside trail upstream back to the bridge. Even though this is a flat section, there are short sections of extremely technical singletrack on offer that require trials-level skills.

Once you reach the entrance of the tunnel again, cross the old railway bridge and turn immediately right down the steep steps to the riverside.

9 Neidpath Castle trail into Peebles

Follow the river downstream on singletrack past Neidpath Castle into the park. Cross another iron bridge over the Tweed and turn left, following the river downstream on the opposite side.

Follow the tarmac footpath downstream to the final challenge. Definitely not for the faint hearted, there is a narrow underpass under the bridge, inches away from the fast-flowing Tweed.

Make sure you walk it or are prepared to float down the final section of this loop which brings you back to Tweed Green.

Options

Easy short cuts & family friendly versions

This route can easily be made beginner-friendly by avoiding the hard climbs and technical singletrack. You'll still have to walk a few sections, but the overall journey involved in this loop is unspoilt:

1 Avoiding the Cademuir Forest Climb

At point 3 ignore the singletrack climb into Cademuir Forest and follow the track straight ahead which contours around the edge of the forest, meeting the forest track once again a the end of the 'Tantah's Trail' descent.

From here you can follow the directions to the switchback descent out of Cademuir Forest.

2 Avoiding Cademuir Ridge

As you exit Cademuir Forest and follow the tarmac road as described in section 4, you can follow the edge of the ridge around to section 6.

As you pass the lone stand of trees, turn right on to the singletrack climb past the trees. Just above the road is a singletrack trail which contours westerly around the ridge. Follow this trail, or the tarmac road, passing the cottages and reaching the picnic area.

3 Avoiding the tunnel and technical Tweedside singletrack

When you reach the entrance of the tunnel in section 7, you can immediately cross the Tweed on the old railway bridge to rejoin the Tweedside singletrack of section 7.

bikefax

Summary

This is one of those rides that seems a lot longer (and a lot harder) than the numbers suggest and despite starting right in the middle of Peebles you'll feel like you're a very long way from civilisation as you're climbing up the slopes of Dollar Law. The ascent here follows 'Thief's Road' – where bandits used to rob unsuspecting travellers – so take care if you've got an expensive bike and don't travel alone.

Once you set off there's no real bail out options, so don't take this ride too lightly as there is absolutely nowhere to stock up on food or water once you get going and not much mobile phone reception.

Definitely a fair weather ride – It's pretty remote in places so take a map and preferably a GPS and know how to use them, as the tracks are sometimes vague and it's not a ride

Peebles

Epic

Moderate

52 km

1551 m

6 - 9 hrs

Landranger 72 & 73

That said, if you like the idea of being out in the wilderness and are confident in your fitness and navigational skills then this is a great ride to do. Thankfully, once at Megget Reservoir the return route offers no real navigational challenges and is a lot quicker than the outward journey, with a fantastic descent coming down from Foulbrig.

Start Point

Start at Pennels Close off the High Street in Peebles (home of Border Bike Sport) and follow the start of the Cademuir ride, crossing over the river Tweed and following signs for the John Buchan Way.

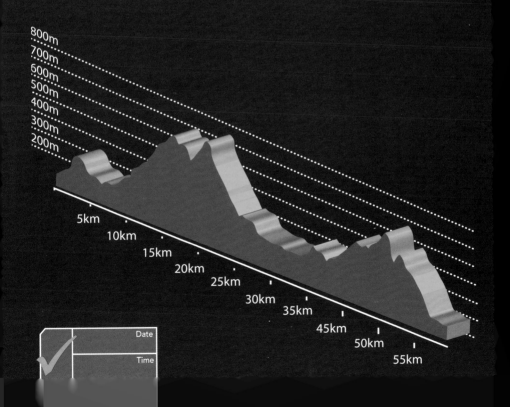

| Date |
| Time |

Peebles

Newby Kipps

Cademuir
Plantation

416

Canada Hill
528

676
Stob Law

R Tweed

A72

Manor Water

300

441

Hall Manor
Woods

B712

200

300

200

200

Ridind Hill
478

Tarcreish

Hopehead Burn

400

300

719
The Scrape

505
Scawd Law

600

500

Route Description

1 Gate

This is where you leave the Cademuir route. Go through the gate bearing right and follow the waymarkers for the John Buchan Way to take you contouring up the hill staying just away from the trees.

2 Fork

Go left, following the John Buchan Way sign and the wall on your left. This wide grassy track can be a very quick descent down to the road. At the road bear right and follow this for 2km where you cross a bridge then take a left at the junction. At the next T junction turn left again following the sign for Manorhead and drop down through the hamlet of Castlehill.

3 Hall Manor Woods

Take the forest track through the gate on your right and start the steady climb upwards. After 1.5km at a junction with a grass track (firebreak), turn right to go steeply uphill. Bear right at the next fork and the track now starts to level out.

4 Dead Wife's Grave

At the edge of the forest there is an old iron gate with one of the stone gate posts simply inscribed 'Dead Wife' (?). Go through the gate and turn left following the fence line uphill through the heather. When the fence turns sharply left up a steep hill bear right on the singletrack that takes an easier gradient contouring around the edge of the hill. This soon joins a doubletrack leading to a gate.

5 Gate

Go through the gate and you're back into the trees. Bear right along a firebreak on a very vague path and a short hike-a-bike section. The path soon joins a double track and becomes rideable again, as long as it's dry.

Once out of the trees the track goes steeply up through the heather to another gate then contours around The Scrape which rises up on your right. Enjoy the isolation, it feels like you're a long way from help – and you are!

When the long section of singletrack eventually peters out, head up hill to the fence line then turn left and follow the fence to the Trig point on Pykestone Hill.

6 Pykestone Hill

Follow the fence line on your right, still heading south. After a short descent, a little climb and another bit of descent you leave the fence and contour around a Long Grain Knowe on a vague grass track. There's a rip-roaring descent just around the corner, taking you down to a shoulder below Dollar Law before a short push up to the cairns.

7 Cairns

After the cairns bear right and cross the fence heading for the obvious grass track that heads up the side of Dollar Law. The track is quite heavy going, with the gradient and grass combining to make a very difficult climb that may have you pushing. You are now in the middle of nowhere!

At the top of the climb head through the gate in the fence and continue in the same direction. Then it's a quick blast down a wide grassy track to reach another gate.

Gate

Go through the gate but ignore the obvious grassy track that heads along the top of the ridge and bear right, going off-piste down through the heather. You should be able to see an obvious surfaced doubletrack below you – aim for that. Once on the track you follow it down (probably very quickly) until it joins the road, where you turn left.

 Track

As the road turns away from the reservoir you will reach a stand of trees on your right. At this point look out for the track on your left, signposted for Manor Water. This stony track takes you relentlessly uphill again for 2km before dropping down to Foulbrig.

10 Foulbrig

After the gate, the track becomes grassy with a short boggy section, before you drop down to a small burn crossing. One last steep pull up and then you have a short contouring section before dropping down to the foot of the glen. The track is an obvious grassy doubletrack all the way, although it rides more like singletrack in truth.

11 Road.

The tarmac only goes in one direction so follow it down the glen for a scenic ride on a very quiet road and by now you're probably glad to be rolling along on the smooth surface.

From Hallmanor Woods simply retrace your outward route, turn right for Peebles at the first junction, then right again following the sign for Peebles via Cademuir at the next junction. Follow the road back to the stand of pine trees on your left and take the track up the hill, following the John Buchan Way markers back into the centre of Peebles.

Variations

This ride could easily be shortened by starting from a number of different places.

Option 1

Megget Reservoir (32 km)

Start the ride at Megget reservoir (WP 9) and turn back at Hallmanor woods (WP 3).

Option 2

Manorhead (32 km)

There's a small parking spot at the end of the road near Manorhead (WP 11). From here, head down the road to pick the trail to Hallmanor woods (WP 3).

Option 3

Drumelzier (44km)

Start from Drumelzier and head straight up to Pykestone Hill (WP 6) to pick up the route. Then at Dead Wife's Grave (WP 4) instead of turning left carry straight on down the hill to pick up the road back to Drumelzier.

Summary

Glentress is undoubtedly the best known of the 7stanes mountain bike centres, and quite rightly so. It has earned its reputation as the premier centre, through the hard work of a lot of people including the folks at the Hub. And the centre continues to develop its facilities, with a growing network of nearly a 100 kilometres of trail all built with excitement and challenge in mind.

This forest combo brings the best of the three main trails together into one tight, technical bag. By heading up the hill on the Red route, taking in the whole of 'Spooky Woods' and then cutting across on the fast and fun 'Betty Blue' on the Blue Trial, to reach the Helly Hansen V Trail at the start of 'Deliverance', you get the best of the singletrack going.

The three trails all have very different characters, from hard packed dirt jumping fun in 'Spooky Woods' on the Red, to

Glentress	
Expert	
Extreme	
16 km	
910 m	
2 - 3 hrs	
Landranger 73	

the narrow, tight, twisty, singletrack of 'Deliverance' on the Black. And it ain't over then! There's still the challenges of the North Shore at 'Ewok Village', the steep and technical on 'Black Dog' and the fast and furious return leg to the Hub.

Getting There

The trail head and the Hub are located two miles east of Peebles on the A72. Arriving from the direction of Peebles, the Visitor Centre is signposted on the left.

Start Point

The route starts from the Forestry Commission Scotland car park at the Hub. You can shorten the route if you want, by starting and finishing it at the Buzzards Nest car park.

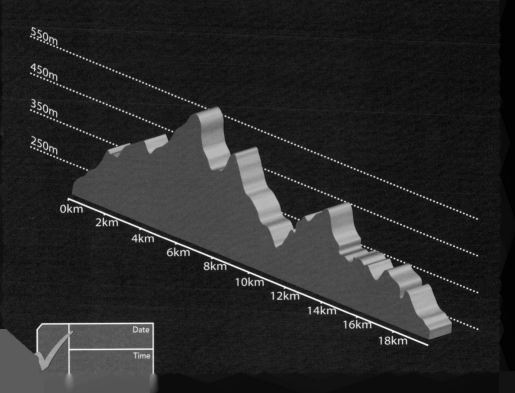

Date
Time

N

Glentress
Forest

Spooky woods

• Caresman Hill
  551

351

2

Betty Blue

Pennels Vennel

1

Kittlegairy Hill

Black Dog

Buzzard's Nest

P

NS

Ewok Village

3

Cardie Hill

350

Linnburn Fm

Falla Brae

Eshiels Hope

P

← Peebles

Eshiels

300

Glentress

Hotel

200

1 km

Route Description

Start at the Hub and follow the Red route markers right to the top and the picnic benches and viewpoint at the start of Spooky Woods. Head down the hill, getting some pretty big air on the first couple of jumps (if that's what you're after) and into the superbly grin inducing Spooky Woods.

1 Post No 43

Look out for Post No 43 at a crossroads and a small hut where the Red crosses doubletrack. Go Left and follow the blue trail through 'Betty Blue'. Sit back and relax on this very fine set of bermed switchbacks, finally popping out on the track ready to set up for 'Deliverance'.

2 Forest Track / Post No 20

At the forest track (Post No 20) turn left, and continue along to Post No 83 and the start of Deliverance. The Deliverance Trail will keep your legs working as you hang on to the saddle to steer the bike delicately through tight narrow singletrack.

At the bottom of Deliverance comes 'Redemption', though not in the form of an easy ride. More in the form of 'what goes down must go back up again'.

Climb the hill of Redemption – time to reflect on the excellence of 'Deliverance'. Then just when you've had enough climbing you'll arrive at Ewok and the North Shore - if that's your bag.

Ewok

Here there are plenty of choices of line and plenty of chicken runs too (just in case!). After Ewok, follow the black markers all the way, with plenty of opportunities to mix and match with the Red on the way back down to the Hub.

Facilities at Glentress

Bike shop
Bike Hire (Including Full suss and DH)
Café
Trail Maps
Showers, changing rooms & toilets

Other routes in Glentress

The Forest has a number of purpose built trails all offering bags of fun

Green	Skills Loop	1.5km
Blue	Buzzards Nest	8km
Blue	The Hub	14km
Red	Red XC	17km
Black	V Trail XC	29km

Freeride

Buzzards Nest Car park
Red, Blue & Black options

More rides in the Tweed Valley

Most people quite naturally associate the Tweed Valley with the forest and trails of Glentress. Hopefully this book has shown that there is a wealth of other stuff out there to be explored in the surrounding countryside.

Here are a few other options that we just couldn't fit into the book. Once you've done all the routes in this book, get an OS map and a maybe a GPS and go out and explore.

Peebles to Gypsy via Glentress
45km Expert

If you're looking for a big day out in the area, and want to get out of the forest and at the same time find some quality riding, this tasty recipe will satisfy all your needs.

Start at Peebles Hydro. Go up the road to follow the track alongside Soonhope Burn and on to the Goat Track. Follow this until you pick up signs for the Black Run at Glentress. Ride up to the Hut on the Black and follow the Black all the way down Britney Spears, Shane McGowan and Deliverance.

Just at the bottom of Deliverance cut left into the clearing and follow vague doubletrack south to Nether Horsburgh Farm and follow the track down to Cardrona.

Cross the main road, pop into Macdonalds Cardrona for posh coffee in their leather sofas and then cross the golf course and the river adn follow the road into Cardrona Forest. From here follow the Gypsy's Descent route description for a cracking descent.

For family riders

There are a number of options in the valley. The Blue route at Glentress offers a slightly harder than usual rider for families and novices and with occasional sharp inclines and fast bermy descents, is better suited to the more active family.

The Green Loop – Glentress

Also in Glentress is the Green Loop which together with the Skills Loop makes for a fun and un-strenuous half day's riding. The Green Loop can be extended by following the forest track on past the start of the Green to take you to the Roundhouse and back to the Green marked trail.

Any version of the Green Loop is best started from the Buzzards Nest Car park.

River Tweed

There are also lots of gentle rides along the Walker Burn and the River Tweed. Pick up a Tweed Trails Leaflet from the Tourist Information Centre in Peebles.

Introduction

With races being held here since before the advent of 'Downhill' as we know it, the hill at Innerleithen is steeped in mountain bike history. Although only five minutes down the road from Glentress, Innerleithen should really be viewed as a completely separate venue in its own right and one for which it is worth putting some time aside for, just because it is so good in it's own right.

To the hardcore, Innerleithen is Project Downhill and with new tracks regularly being cut in for the SDA series mixing with the old favourites such as the Cresta Run and sponsored tracks such as the already revered Matador, there are plenty of options all round.

The Matador double black is everything that the downhiller aspires to. Huge drop offs, enormous berms and cheeky gap jumps, all smile temptingly at you on the way up, but then have a habit of snarling menacingly on the way down. Heading down the other side of the hill, 'Make or Break' is a more manageable red graded version, but netherthless huge' huge, fun with its long fast flowing sections of berms and jumps.

Food & Drink

There are two small grocery shops in the village. We like Malik's slightly eccentric store, at the bottom of the road to the forest (he does some organic stuff as well as the usual). En route to the tracks is the Traquair Arms Hotel which does all -day food, either outside with the bike, or inside in their very contemporary bar. Down the High Street there is also the Corner House Hotel which boasts food and the 7 Spices takeaway. If this isn't enough for you drive 5 minutes and you'll be in Peebles or the café at the Hub.

Accommodation

Innerleithen is just ten minutes drive from Peebles. so all the same B&B's and hotels as mentioned in the Peebles introduction can be just as handy for a stay here.

Right opposite the road to the tracks is The Bike Lodge, www.thebikelodge.co.uk, a self catering independent hostel for mountain bikers run by Nic, an enthusiastic DH and XC junkie and mechanic at the Hub.

If it's hotels and B&B you are looking for then the Traquair Arms Hotel offers contemporary style in a traditional hotel and is fully mountain bike savvy.

In Selkirk

There are two bunkhouses here, Broadmeadows YHA, and along the Yarrow Valley, The Gordon Inn. The Gordon Inn also does good food and beer.

Websites & Info

www.sda-races.com
www.descent-world.co.uk
www.gravity-slaves.co.uk
www.sda-races.com
www.redbullprojectdownhill.co.uk

Summary

Both the Matador and the Cresta Run start at the top of Plora Rig. For the Cresta Run, continue right to the end of the ascent path to the Starting Box and for the Matador, keep going upwards at the last bend in the ascent path.

The Matador

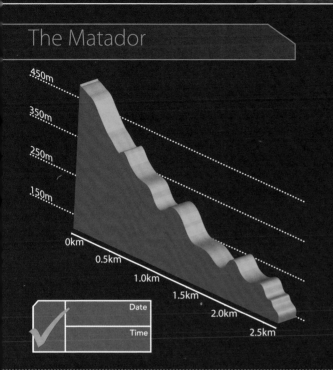

450m
350m
250m
150m

0km
0.5km
1.0km
1.5km
2.0km
2.5km

Date
Time

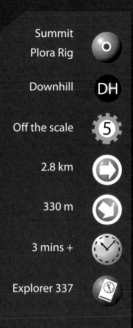

Summit
Plora Rig

Downhill — DH

Off the scale — 5

2.8 km

330 m

3 mins +

Explorer 337

The Cresta Run

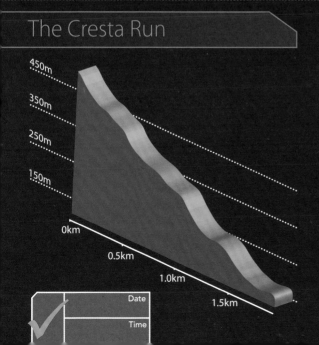

450m
350m
250m
150m

0km
0.5km
1.0km
1.5km

Date
Time

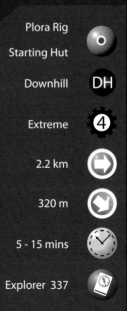

Plora Rig
Starting Hut

Downhill — DH

Extreme — 4

2.2 km

320 m

5 - 15 mins

Explorer 337

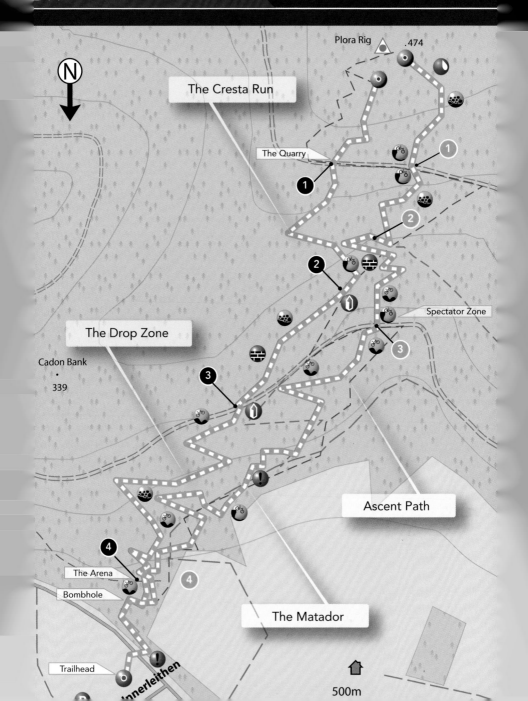

N

Plora Rig △ .474

The Cresta Run

The Quarry

1

1

2

2

Spectator Zone

The Drop Zone

3

Cadon Bank
·
339

3

Ascent Path

4

The Arena

Bombhole

4

The Matador

Trailhead

Innerleithen

500m

Summary: The Matador

Summary: Cresta Run

A real mix of off the scale drops, jumps, and gaps, fast natural lines and crazy technical rock gardens. All the 'bad boys' have chicken runs down the side, but just ride it and grasp at the dream of being able to take the whole thing clean.

This is the 'baddest' of all the DH here (for the moment at least) and a superb adrenaline filled 5 minutes of riding with everything from fast rocky sections to technical tight roots and plenty of air filled moments on some well built monster drops. Session the bad bits and then nail it all in a oner.

To see video footage of the course take a look at www.bloodsweatngears.co.uk

If you have a fondness for 'old school' DH riding, then you will love this. The lines are fast, steep and tight with a natural feel to them. The Cresta Run weaves its constricted technical switchbacking self through trees, over roots and into the gloom with a good deal of attitude. Expect to be brushing shoulders with a fair number of trees and don't underestimate the sudden tightness of the corners. There are no man-made berms here to spin you out - too much speed and you'll be cutting your own tracks .

Combine the Cresta Run and the Drop Zone for a full on super technical and rooty track . Dont expect any let up all the way from top to bottom .

To get to the start of the DH

1 Best way up is definitely to go on a day when there is an Uplift Service. If you do this you'll be deposited on the track next to the Quarry. From here go back on yourself for about 100 metres and then push up the well signposted path up to the summit of Plora Rig.

2 If sadly there's no uplift, then it'll have to be heads down for a bit of a push. This will take you about 45 minutes to the top. From the car park follow the markers for the Traquair and follow the trail all the way up till it meets up with the first forest track (you can ride all of this). Turn left here and go along for about 200m (passing the awesome jumps on the Black) until you see a wide path going up diagonally rightwards. Push up this to another forest road. Turn left here and go past the Quarry to a well signposted path on the right which leads to the start of all the tracks.

3 If you don't want to go all the way to the top there are plenty of opportunities on the way up to session various bits of tracks.

DH The Matador

The track starts innocently enough with a wide heathery trail, but after just 100m it shows its true colours as it narrows down, weaves around to the left and then right again for a fast traverse with some peddling across the hillside and then into the trees.

Here it gets rutted and rooty and at times a bit wet. Three rock steps take you down and back round into a fast straight before hitting a rocky ramp and a big jump with a good landing.

Occasional black arrows on yellow signs reassure you that you are still on track. Rocks and trees set up a crazy slalom course for a period with drops and jumps off roots. After this the track takes the fall line, then some off camber action and watch out for the big steep rocky ramp down to the forest track.

1 Fire Road

Take the jump (loose landing), as you cross the forest track and fast back into the trees. Here the line gets loose and narrow. Float over the ball bearing like surface to a couple of small stepdowns with the smoothest line on the right taking you down to the bridleway.

2 Bridleway

Turn right and then left off the path after 50 metres and down to a big jump with a good landing onto a wide section of track (chicken run down the right hand side of the jump). Head left through a gap in the wall and down loose ground with small steps to come back through the wall and heading right.

A narrow line takes you straight down through the trees and then opens into a 2 metre wide section with two big doubles leading into the huge drop off and berm to the fire road.

This is the spectator zone with a photographer's gallery off to your left. Throw yourself off the drop and hang what seems like forever in the air. Alternatively check it out and take the chicken run down the right hand side with two smaller drops into the berm.

3 Fire Road

Cross the fire road and style it spectacularly on the jumps and doubles on the other side. Then continue through a series of jumps, berms, small step downs and doubles and back into the trees.

Here a choice of lines with a tight technical line up on the bank on the right and a smoother line down left. Both finish with a gap jump across a wide path (with the usual chicken run off right) and then a short steep bit of loose dirt to a path again and out of the conifers and into natural woodland.

Head off rightwards and into a small gap jump or a smooth line through on the right. A long traverse takes you into a set of tabletops with a berm taking you out of it.

4 The Arena

Track and footpath converge at the Arena sign. A worn rooty line leads through the trees and with a couple of small steps into the infamous Bombhole. Fly out of this and into the berms with a couple of hero jumps to finish.

DH The Cresta Run

Start

At Plora Rig. Continue past 'Make or Break' for another 50 m to the starting box by the wall.

Start in the box and take the left line out of the starting hut.

The trail splits immediately with the red and green versions of the Red Bull going off rightwards in the trees. What starts easily, soon degenerates into twisting narrow switchbacks and rutted tracks. Keep to the left track as it takes a thin line through the trees. Switchback through the trees and drop onto the forest track.

1 'Cresta Run Middle' sign

Cross the forest track (a sign indicates the way) and drop in to a traversing track which soon switchbacks back left. A loose, rutted line crossed by worn roots provides plenty of interest with a series of natural drop offs on bends caused by eroded roots and stumps.

2 Ascent Path

Tight singletrack drops you steeply onto the ascent trail. Turn right and follow it for 100m down from where the Red Bull crosses. At the Red Bull 'green' sign go right along a fast rocky section, through a gap in the wall and on with one last switchback to the forest track.

3 Drop Zone

At the Cadon Bank fire road straight opposite you is 'the Drop Zone', and right again, 'Another Brick in the Wall'. For the best combo, go straight on down the Drop Zone for tight twisting technical fun.

The Drop Zone starts on fast smooth dirt only to suddenly deteriorate into the same worn loose surface you've come to expect on this track. A set of jumps and rock step downs lead into an area where anything goes.

Now the track turns straight down the fall line, loose and dirty, to cross the path and arrive at the Arena. Finish on more loose rooty stuff, or straight ahead for the bombhole and berms.

If you want to start on something a bit more forgiving than either the Matador or the Cresta Run, then head for the start of the DH tracks at the top of Plora Rig and take your pick of whole bag options including the original Red Bull or the Hub's own track 'Make or Break'. Technical 'old school' DH riding on the Red Bull and the Deerhunter contrasts nicely withthe groomed, bermed and perfectly angled jumps of the Hub school of trail building on 'Make or Break'.

Start Points

The start points of these two rides are at the top of Plora Rig close to the start of the Cresta Run and the Matador. Head for the top of Plora Rig and look out for signboards marking the starts of these two routes.

Red Bull

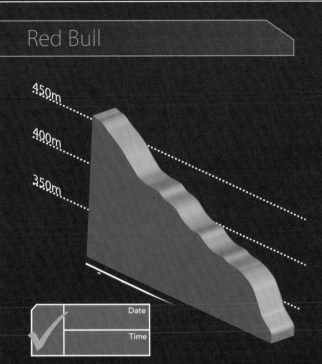

450m
400m
350m

Plora Rig	
Downhill	DH
Hard	3
1.9 km	
3 - 15 mins	
Landranger 73	

	Date
✓	Time

'Make or Break'

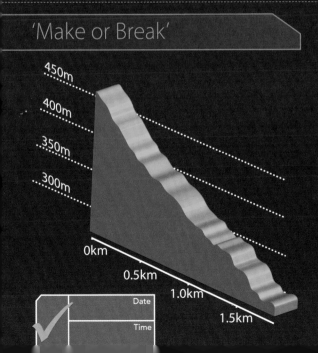

450m
400m
350m
300m

0km
0.5km
1.0km
1.5km

Plora Rig	
Downhill	DH
Hard	DH
1.9 km	
3 - 15 mins	
Landranger 73	

	Date
✓	Time

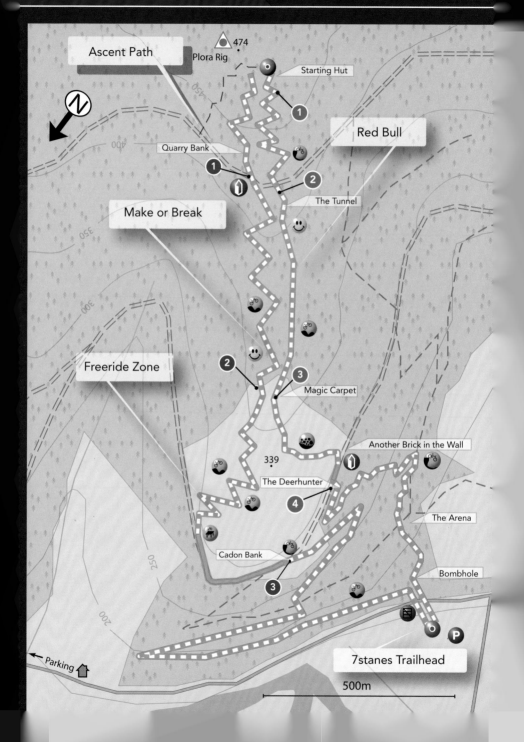

Ascent Path

474
Plora Rig

Starting Hut

Red Bull

Quarry Bank

The Tunnel

Make or Break

Freeride Zone

Magic Carpet

Another Brick in the Wall

339

The Deerhunter

The Arena

Cadon Bank

Bombhole

7stanes Trailhead

Parking

500m

 Red Bull

Right, let's get one thing straight; when these trails were built nobody was riding downhill rigs with 8 inches of front and rear travel. 'Back in the day' those bikes just didn't exist. So, if you've got any amount of suspension on your bike and a decent amount of technical skills you'll be able to ride these lines, if you've got a long travel DH bike you'll probably be able to ride them a bit quicker and spend some more time in the air.

If you like technical XC riding, or "old school downhill" then you're going to love this, just be sure to drop your saddle before you set off - it'll help you stay on the bike and might stop the downhillers laughing at you (maybe).

Body Armour and a full face helmet might also be a good idea - if you do come off the chances are you'll hit a tree or a rock. In fact, the safest option would be to stay at home and watch TV, don't even think about riding this trail.

To sum it up in a word: rooty.

'Make or Break'

So many trails have been cut in here over the years, that you'll often find tracks confusingly known by several names. This can make trails hard to identify. 'Make or Break' (also known as the Hub Line trail), though, is easy to identify by the big white sign boards at the start.

Built on a long history of downhilling at Innerleithen and with all the knowledge gained from designing and operating the trails at Glentress, this track is most definitely 'new school'. Tightly packed with berms huge sweeping switchbacks, jumps, doubles and table tops with front faces so steep you could almost fall off backwards, the trail is fast exhilarating and challenging.

You can session the trail, or pop out at Cador Bank, turn left and head straight down the last section of the Traquiar XC trail, for bombholes berms and a series of ever steeper, deeper and faster, step downs.

This is not a technical track, though there is plenty to keep your wits about you for. In the main it's wide, smooth, fairly forgiving and ideal to have a go at if you're new to downhilling or pushing yourself into doing jumps.

Red Bull

1 Roots Manoeuvres

The Green & Red start together from the Hut at the top of Plora Rig. There are two lines going into the trees at the start. Take the wide, rooty trail on the right. This very quickly forks, but they both end up on the fire road at pretty much the same spot so it doesn't matter which line you take There are at least four variations you can take from here down to the lay-by on the fire road and they are all fairly similar in character. Session them all to find your favourite one!

Go left and the wide, muddy, rooty trail becomes narrow and loose as it twists down through the trees.

Take the right fork and bounce your way down, over and around the roots. Where the track forks again go right for more roots and chutes and look out for the sharp left turn that leads you down to a jump at the fire road lay-by.

2 The Tunnel

If you took the left line down to this point you'll want to go right for 20 metres at the fire road to pick up the next section. If you hit the jump with enough speed you won't even touch the fire road!

Back into the trees, the next section goes dead straight for about 200m on a wide track with more roots, but not as technical as before.

3 Magic Carpet sign

When you come into a cleared area the "'Make or Break' trail is clearly visible about 3m to your right.

At the "Magic Carpet" sign the trail forks. The wide grassy track on the left turns into bermed switchbacks, in the style of Spooky Woods a Glentress, while the track on the right is a bi spicier.

Narrow singletrack starts off snaking its wa down parallel to 'Make or Break' before swooping left into a fast, tight section with a few small steps (all rollable). Just watch ou for the mini rock garden. A right hander drops you onto the second fire road.

4 Cadon Bank / The Deerhunter

You can go right here and 200m down the fire road brings you to the top of Cadon Bank descent if you need another fix of that. Or do the old skool Deerhunter line right in front o you - very tight and technical with some trick switchbacks, again all just about rollable The further down you go the steeper it gets so if you didn't drop your saddle at the top you'll be on the ground in a heap somewhere around here.

Try not to hit any trees as you snake you way down negotiating the steps, roots and switchbacks. After some more loose, rutted and twisty fun you're into "The Arena", the final stretch.

With a myriad of line choices where you can start stylin' it for the crowds that you can easily imagine standing awestruck at your mad skillz Enjoy the berms at the bottom and don' forget to stop before you hit the road.

DH 'Make or Break'

Start

Head straight into the gloom of the dense trees at the start and straight off it'sfast furious fun on hardpacked brown dirt, with small jumps, berms and switchbacks. The track is plenty wide and is probably the easiest line hereabouts.

1 Fire Road

Almost as suddenly as you entered the trees, you are back out of them and crossing the road just next to 'The Quarry' for another section of berms and high speed thrilling entertainment.

2 Magic Carpet

An exit from the trees and a pause for breath gives you a moment to appreciate the breathtaking scenery hereabouts. The next section, the Magic Carpet truly is a magical experience that will have you feeling like you are floating down the hillside, with its broad sweeping berms, generous jumps and doubles and beautifully crafted tabletops.

3 Cadon Bank

Turn left at the track and go along for 100 metres to the start of the Cadon Bank section of the Traquair XC Trail. This section can be very intimidating to the uninitiated. Take a look at the downside of the jumps before you ride them, they are all rollable, and its worth doing them a couple of times if you are new to jumps as it will build your confidence no end.

Once you've started on this section, it just carries on down, and down, and down, until finally it's back into the trees for one last furious section of bombholes and jumps.

bikefax

Traquair XC Trail

Innerleithen

Summary

The people who put this trail together have done an astoundingly good job of welding a whole heap of different elements together and making it flow in a truly memorable and enjoyable manner. Interest is aroused early on with the rock steps and clever little rock slaloms on the initial ascent, followed much, much, much later on with the superb 'Plora Craig' section where tight trials moves come only after you are well and truly warmed up.

In between these are plenty of traditional narrow heathery singletrack and a peak baggers delight – Minch Moor with its 360 degree views of the surrounding hills. And all this is finished off with a truly yeehah descent over a huge series of bomb holes, berms, drops and rollers. If you're not smiling by the time you finish this ride, you need to see a dentist!

Innerleithen

Expert

Extreme

20 km

500 m

2 - 4 hrs

Landranger 73

Getting there

From Innerleithen High Street, take the turn off at the church, signposted '7stanes Downhill Project'. Go straight down the road, past the Traquair Hotel and over a narrow, traffic lighted bridge. The Trail Head is the just after this on the left.

Start Point

Start at the 7stanes trail head car park. Trail Head facilities? Not a lot! A big car park and 2 Portaloos and that's it at the moment. So pick up some grub and spares before you get there.

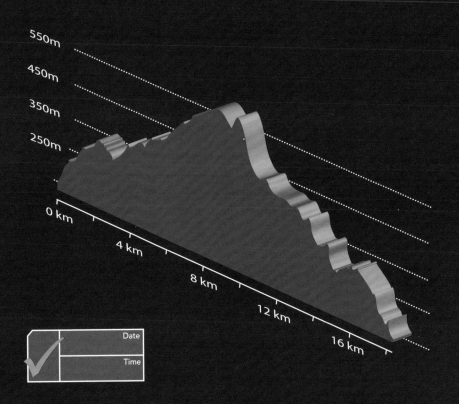

Date	
Time	

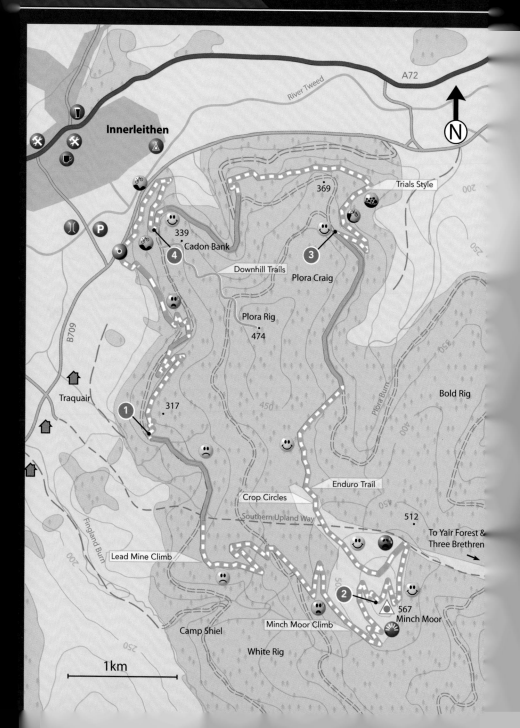

A72

River Tweed

Innerleithen

369

Trials Style

339

Cadon Bank

4

Downhill Trails

Plora Craig

3

Plora Rig

474

B709

Traquair

317

450

Plora Burn

Bold Rig

1

Enduro Trail

Crop Circles

512

To Yair Forest &
Three Brethren

Southern Upland Way

Fingland Burn

Lead Mine Climb

2

567

Minch Moor

Camp Shiel

Minch Moor Climb

White Rig

1km

N

XC Route Description

There's no gentle start to this route, some of the steepest climbing on the route comes right at the start, so take a few turns around the car park before you start, or grit your teeth for the inevitable burn in the calf muscles.

After you've headed up through the Spectator's Spot the trail starts to ease, then doubling back on itself enters some entertaining steps and rock slaloms. You can never say the climbing on this route is dull.

1 Taniel Hill Quarry

After this section, flowing contouring singletrack drops you into the Taniel Hill gravel quarry, where three options beckon – easy to the left, medium in the middle, or real, real steep on the right. Take your pick, then stay a while and play or turn left on the fire road and start the ascent to Minch Moor.

If bagging the summit ain't your thing, look out for the short cut, which will cut you across the hillside avoiding the summit.

2 Minch Moor

Minch Moor summit is worth the effort once you get there. With 360 degree views of the surrounding hills.

After your fill of views, bermy singletrack snakes you eastwards down the hillside. At the bottom of this a surprise re-ascent almost takes you back up to the summit, but then drops you back down the hill again. Check out the strange crop circles at 'Resolution Point'. The mystery will be revealed when you get there.

Ride through the crop circles on tight fast singletrack, dropping onto a fire road and a short opportunity to casually wander along looking at the views and figuring where the hell you are.

3 Elibank Forest

A metal barrier and a signpost pointing you down right through the brash leads you innocently at first in to the penultimate section of trail. The 7 stanes map warns that 'Plora Craig' contains 'impossible' trials style sections. As the trail hots up, tight little wiggles through stumps and boulders gradually increase the tempo, and even when you think its all over and getting easy again, don't put the saddle back up, 'cos there's still more.

4 Cadon Bank

A brief session on fire road takes you over to Cadon Bank and the spot some of the DH trails cross over. A hundred metres further on and the black plummets off the side of the trail for the final descent.

Technical rock steps on a steep hillside get you started followed by a never ending string of ever deepening bomb holes. From here on it's freeride all the way to the bottom, with a big jump in an open section just before the finish, just to make sure you look good in front of the crowds in the car park…

You'll want to come back and do it even better and even faster the second, and third, and fourth time…

Innerleithen

Summary

The Minch Moor Road is a well known old drover's road that provides an off-road link from Traquair forest and Innerleithen over to Yarrowfod and if you wish, onwards to Selkirk. You'll find no real navigational challenges on this ancient track, just a big climb, big views and an even bigger descent. The only thing that's not big is the distance, at a modest 24 kilometres.

If the idea of such a climb fills you with fear then you can reassure yourself that there's plenty of rest spots at the gates on the Minch Moor Road and again as you follow the Old Drove Road across the tops to the giant cairns of the Three Brethren.

And even if you are a 'King of the Mountains', it's worth stopping to admire the view once in a while.

Flotterstone	
Classic	
2 with short sections of 3	
24 km	
675 m	
2 - 3 hrs	
OS Explorer 344	

Getting there

Selkirk is the meeting point for a number of roads, making it accessible from every direction. The A7 runs north to Galashiels (6 miles) and south to Hawick (11 miles).

The A707 heads north-west up the Tweed Valley to Innerleithen (15 miles) and the A708 heads south-west to Moffat (34 miles).

Start Point

From Selkirk head out of town on the A708 towards St. Mary's Loch and Moffat for an easy spin on the road down to Yarrowford.

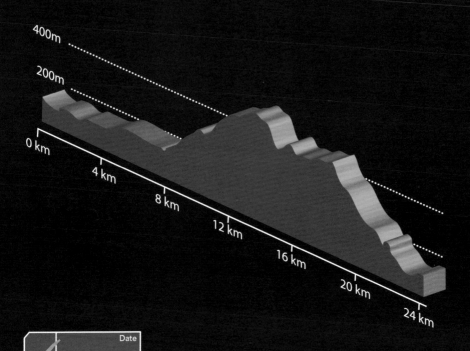

	Date
	Time

Brown
Knowe
523

3

Cairn
452

4

Yair Hill Forest

Minchmoor Road

Hangingshaw Burn

Three Brethren

6

Whitehope
Rig
325

463
Broomy
Law

5

Lewenshope Rig

2

Foulshiels
Hill
444

Long Phillip Burn

Hanginshaw

Yarrowford

1

Black Andrew Wood

Moffat

Yarrow Water

200

250

300

300

400

450

Hareh

324

Bowhill

1km

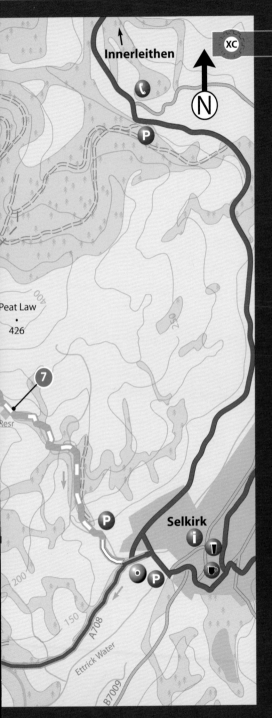

Route Description

1 Yarrowford

Just after the phone box turn right following the signpost for "Innerleithen via the Minch Moor". Follow the road past the row of timber garages where it turns into a track, then immediately turn right and continue uphill for 100m.

As the track levels out take the hairpin turn on your left (before you reach the trees) then when you join another track turn right up a steep challenging climb to a gate. Go through the gate and turn left on the grassy track, following the "Tweed Trails" waymarkers, keeping the wall on your left.

2 Gate

At the 3rd gate, the wall you've been following comes to an end and the track bears right, follow it uphill keeping the fence to your right. The grassy track is obvious - its the only one and it goes relentlessly uphill!

3 Southern Upland Way

Turn right when you reach the Southern Upland Way signpost. You think you're at the top, but there's still more climbing up to the cairn, although the gradient is much easier now. Once through the gate you can blast on down the stone track. Hardtail riders will feel every stone on the trail here, while full-suss riders can just sit down and enjoy the view.

4 Gate

Carry straight on, following the sign for Broadmeadows Youth Hostel. The track is grassy now and gives you a gentle climb before dropping down to another gate with a huge mast on your right. Now follow the wall on your right until you get to the trees.

5 Bench

When you get to the trees, go through the gate and you'll find a bench where you can stop to enjoy an energy gel or a pork pie. From here follow the obvious doubletrack, keeping the trees on your left. There's a stiff climb up to the Three Brethren – the impressively huge stone cairns.

6 Three Brethren

Take a right just past the Three Brethren (don't cross the fence) following the SUW markers down through the heather on a very fast descent. Hit the brakes as you go through a pair of fence posts because you turn right here going through a gate and taking the surfaced doubletrack ahead of you that goes down the hill.

This doubletrack soon becomes a boulder fest where the trail has been washed out, but there's a rideable line to the right, just don't fall in the gully.

At the junction at the bottom go left on the wide track which is loose, rocky and fast, then becoming grassy, rocky and fast (just for a change).

7 Reservoir

Go through the gate following the wall on your left. It's pretty much downhill from here. Ignore the right turn (you're probably going too fast to make it anyway) and carry on down the doubletrack until it comes out at a wide parking area. From here take the tarmac road on the right and at the next junction go straight across, heading back into Selkirk on the same route you started on.

More rides

Innerleithen, Selkirk, Galashiels, Jedburgh, Newcastleton and the Cheviots! Yes, there is an awful lot of both traditional and waymarked trail riding to do in this area.

Selkirk & Innerleithen

As well as all the marked trails in the Traquair Forest at Innerleithen, there is plenty or exploring potential to be had by riders with an OS map and a responsible attitude, out on the open slopes of Broomy Law off the Minch Moor road.

Pete Laing, local trail guru, is currently working on a project to link Innerleithen to Selkirk with a waymarked trail and he hopes that this could really open up this area for mountain bike riders.

Newcastleton

Newcastleton, another of the 7stanes centres, is largely aimed at family & novice riders, but with lots of trail building action going on, it's worth keeping an eye on the site.

The forest is located just north east of Carlisle. To get there head to Bonchester Bridge and Newcastleton village on the B6357, then take the unclassified road at south end of Newcastleton and follow the 7stanes signs.

The forest has 5 waymarked trails: the Skills Trail, The Caddrouns, The Linns. Red Trail, and Black Ridge.

For more info:
www.7stanes.gov.uk

Jedburgh The Justice Trail 40km

Another of Pete Laing's trail contributions, the Justice trail was built in conjunction with local riders at Jedburgh. The Trail links together 'ancient drovers' roads, winding singletrack with 'lung bursting climbs'. Start point is the main town car park next to the Visitor Information Centre in town. Pick up maps at the Visitor Centre.

For more information:

www.jedforesttrails.org
www.therush.uk.com

The Cheviots

Whilst there is lots of controversy in Southern Scotland about what region actually constitutes 'the Borders', this area, undoubtedly, is 'The Border'. There is a whole host of cross border rides and the rides along the Cheviot ridge itself can be outstanding on a fair weather day.

Windy Gyle 29km

Just to the south east of Jedburgh, the small village of Twoford is the start of a very fine track up onto the Cheviot ridge and the summit of Windy Gyle (619m). The ride in pretty stiff in places, and the paved flagstone sections on the ridge will test your riding skills at times. From Twoford, head up the track to Blackhall Hill. Turn left here to follow the ridge as far as Windy Gyle (a visit to the summit is optional), and then head off left to follow signs to Hownam for a great descent down 'The Street'. At Hownam, head left and head back along the road to pick up your car.

15

14

16

Thornhill

Dumfries

Wanlockhead

17

Moffat

18

Lowther Mission	14	XC
Drumlanrig	15	XC
Death on the Hills	16	XC
Durisdeer Loop	17	XC
Ae DH	18	DH

Introduction

With three of the 7stanes centres within its boundaries, Dumfries-shire is the first place you are likely to hit if you are doing a Scottish road trip. Ae forest, Dalbeattie and Mabie as well as Drumlanrig and the Lowther hills are all tightly concentrated into this one small region. With all this, it's quite likely you won't get any further north first time round.

Dumfriesshire is an area of riding contrasts with everything from mad slabs at Dalbeattie, secret singletrack at Mabie, full face DH action at Ae, posh trails at Drumlanrig Castle and wide open moorland ranges of the Lowther Hills. Bring all the kit you've got cos you're likely to use it all.

Getting there

From the North

Head down the M74 to Moffat (J15) and the A701 for Dumfries, or for riding in the north of the region, head off at J14 at Elvanfoot.

From the South

For Southerners it's a case of jumping on the delightful M6 and driving north as far as the motorway will take you. When it turns into the A74, continue on as far as Gretna (J22) and turn off onto the A75 for Dumfries.

Food & Drink

As the county town, Dumfries is the biggest metropolis in the area and so has plenty of services for when you are not riding. There's a Tesco on the A76 exit of the A75 if you're self catering and need to stock up. For eating out the Pancake Place on English Street is a good fill up spot. Or for a good pre-ride bacon roll, Rico's next to G & G cycles is highly recommended. There's no end of choice for food and drink in Dumfries in the evenings and a wander around will always find something to suit every preference.

This is also where Robert Burns spent most of his days and the Burns Centre in the town of Dumfries tells his story as well as having a café, film theatre and restaurant.

The smaller neighbouring town of Castle Douglas, just south of the A75, is known as the food town of Dumfries and Galloway. Go there at the right time of year and you might find yourself participating in a food festival – which probably won't do your biking career much good!!

There is a Tesco store (not 24 hr) as you come into the town from the east and loads of eateries down the high street. Try 'The Scottish Pantry', for good old fashioned grub or 'Designs Café' for organic food and quality lavezzo coffee. Just out of town the Laurie Arms at Hough of Urr does outstanding food in the evenings.

If you are around Dalbeattie and looking for something to eat, pop into the 'Little Treat' in the middle of the High Street for good down to earth grub. There's also Mambo's which does a good takeaway (everything from pizza to baguettes) just along the High Street.

At Mabie forest, there's a small café located next to the hire centre, or if this is closed, turn right out on the main road and head up the road for just a couple of minutes to the CriffelInn for a proper bike friendly pub.

In the north of the region, if you're up at

Drumlanrig or in the Lowther Hills, there's always the snack bar or slightly more upmarket tea rooms at Drumlanrig Castle as well as plenty of hotel and cafes lining the small town of Thornhill. If you're riding in the Lowthers then the best welcome is to be found at the Visitor Centre café at Wanlockhead.

Accommodation

For well located accommodation in a small hotel, you can't beat the Criffel Inn at New Abbey just on the edge of Mabie Forest. Owned by ex pro DH racer, Clive Forth, you not only get good food and accommodation you can also get the lowdown on the best trails around. www.criffelinn.com

Bike friendly B&B's in the area include: Wallamhill B&B in Kirkton just outside Dumfries (www.wallamhill.co.uk) and the friendly family run Dalbeattie B&B (www.dalbeattieguesthouse.co.uk).

For self catering there's plenty to choose from depending on whereabouts you want to locate yourself. Bike friendly places include Barnsoul Farm, www.barnsoulfarm.co.uk, in Shawhead,. Camping at Barnsoul Farm is a real treat, with acres of fields and woodlands to spread out in.

Also just outside Dumfries and well located for all the southern 7stanes is Barend Holiday Village at Sandyhills, www.barendholidayvillage.co.uk with picturesque log cabins and a heated pool. Redcastle Cottages, www.redcastlecottages.co.uk, are also just a few miles from Dalbeattie and Castle Douglas and close to the Laurie Arms.

For more ideas on where to stay visitsouthernscotland has a comprehensive list of accommodation providers in the area.

Bike shops and hire

G & G Cycle Centre, 10-12 Academy Street, Dumfries, have a good selection of hire bikes, form dirt jumpers to XC. tel 01387 259483 www.cycle-centre.com As this book goes to print they are also just in the process of setting up a hire centre and shop at 'The Shed' in Mabie Forest. Check out their web site for more details.

Castle Douglas Cycle Centre is a little further west and the last bike shop before Kirroghtree and Glentrool. They do a friendly repair and service as well as stock a host of spares. Located just off the High Street on Church Street. Tel 01556 504542 www.cdbikes.co.uk

Rick Alsop is a legend around these parts and Rik's Bike Shed at Drumlanrig Castle is worth a visit, not just for Rik' expert mechanical services, hire and shop but also to see the eccentric collection of old bikes including a replica of the first ever bicycle made by Kirkpatrick Macmillan in 1840.

More info

Castle Douglas Tourist info centre is in the car park just past Tesco's on the left as you come into the town 01556 253862.

Dumfries TIC is next to the river between the two bridges, tel: 01387 253862

www.visitdumfriesandgalloway.co.uk

www.dgaccommodation.co.uk

www.visitsouthwestscotland.com

www.forestry.gov.uk/forestry

www.visitsouthernscotland.com

www.touristnetuk.com/Sc/dumfries

www.buccleuch.com

Lowther Mission

Dumfriesshire

Summary

Away from the beautifully-groomed singletrack of Drumlanrig, this route seems fairly modest for an epic at a little over 50km. This is definitely not a ride to be underestimated however. This ride has the habit of sucking up your whole day, no matter when you set out - partly because the scenery demands constant viewing, and partly because of the acid-inducing climbs and not to forget the great wee café at Wanlockhead.

Make sure you don't set off on this ride too late, because you'll want to catch the café when it's open and take the time to digest the tasty food before the third large climb of the ride.

The route heads north from Drumlanrig up the fast-flowing River Nith and into the Lowther Hills through 'bike n hike' territory. If you are feeling fit, the first half of this ride is a

Drumlanrig	
Epic	
Hard	
60 km	
1500 m	
7 - 11 hrs	
Landranger 78	

challenge to behold. Those with hangovers, best get a head start. The last third of this ride is what you'll remember though. A seemingly endless descent on a tiny ribbon of singletrack with a big drop below is enough to make you forget all the climbing it took to get the reward. The Enterkin Pass is a real gem to ride, and starting and finishing at a Castle with great trails isn't that bad either.

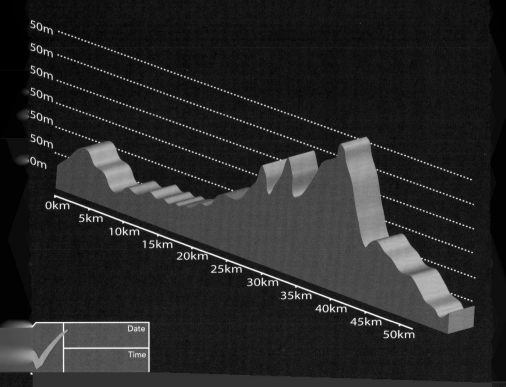

Getting there

Drumlanrig Castle is 20 miles north of Dumfries train station, or 40 miles south-east of Kilmarnock on the A76. You can also reach Drumlanrig on the A702 60 miles south-west of Edinburgh.

Start Point

Drumlanrig Castle. Hire bikes, maps and advice available from Rik's Bike Shed (01848 330080). Car parking costs around a fiver for the day.

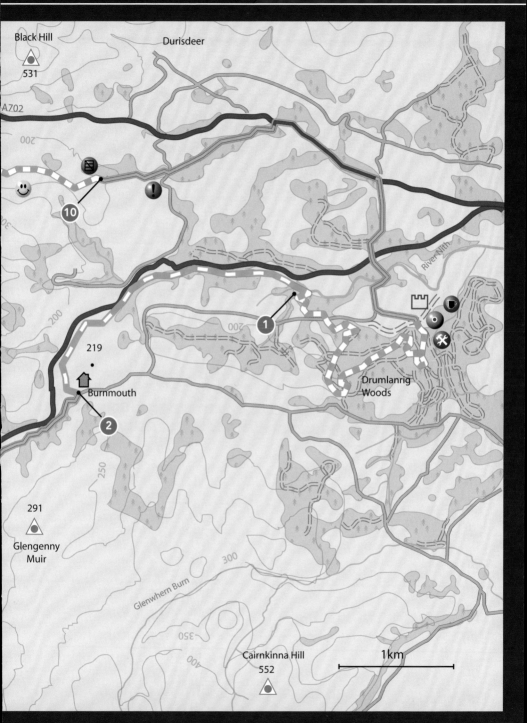

Black Hill

531

Durisdeer

A702

200

10

200

300

200

1

219

Burnmouth

2

250

291

Glengenny
Muir

300

Glenwhern Burn

350

400

Cairnkinna Hill

552

Drumlanrig
Woods

River Nith

1km

Route Description

River Nith

Follow the doubletrack north alongside the river. Go through the metal gate with the flowery house on your right and continue on the manicured grass. Don't worry – you're not about to arrive in someone's back garden! Continue into farmland across a gate. The trail is vague in places, but maintain your distance from the river and resist the temptation to climb the hill on your left. After 5.5km of following the Nith from Dr Evil, you reach a descent to a road after a farm.

2 Burnmouth

Turn right on the road and continue as it winds its way through intermittent houses for another 5km. After 1km, ensure you turn left to stay on the B-road and avoid joining the main A76. This is a gentle climb. At the end of the B-road you find yourself pointing on to the A76. Turn right and follow the pavement for 1 km through Mennock

3 Mennock

Shortly after Mennock turn left across the bridge onto the B797 towards Wanlockhead. After just over 1km into the climb, turn left over the narrow bridge and climb up the gravel road. This is a 1km climb to Auchentaggart Farm. Turn left in the farm and cross through a series of gates over 4 km to Bogg. This is a bleak moor, but look around at the panoramic views of Nithsdale.

4 Bogg

Turn right shortly after the cottage at Bogg.

Now you are on to the Southern Upland Way (SUW), which you follow all the way to Wanlockhead. After half a km on gravel road, you turn left onto a grassy climb. Here is the first big bike 'n' hike challenge of the day – a 1.5km grassy climb up to a saddle for the first reward of the day.

From the saddle, cross the fence and descend towards the woodland at Cogshead. This descent is of the 'how fast dare you go' type and there are plenty of grassy bumps to keep you holding on tight. As you near the woods there is a sharp left hand turn through a gate on to the forest road.

5 Cogshead

Turn right, descending on the forest road, shortly thereafter the Southern Upland Way splits and you take the right turn towards the ruined croft at Cogshead. In what feels like a mirror image of the previous grassy climb/descend, turn left and follow the Southern Upland Way up and over towards Glengaber Hill.

There are some short technical stream crossings to test you on this long gradual climb. After nearly 2km of height-gain you reach another fence denoting the start of the descent. Again, this is a 'dare you' descent with some nice banked corners. Take a dip through the river crossing at the bottom and turn right towards Wanlockhead.

6 Wanlockhead

Heading up the valley towards Scotland's highest village, you pass through ruined 18th century lead mines which are reflected in a lot of the local place names. After the previous hairy descent, take the time to wind down and soak in your surroundings on the cruise into the village. As you hit the main road through the village, cross over to the Mining museum café and enjoy some good food.

 Lowther Hill

From Wanlockhead there are a couple of options. The SUW heads offroad up to the summit of Lowther hill, 300m further above the village. However to let your lunch digest, head north-east on the main road through the village as it winds steeply uphill past the miners' library.

Cross over the B797 to the Lowther Hill access road which leads up to the air traffic control aerial masts. This long winding road is the last climb of the day, setting you up for the Enterkin Pass descent. There are a series of masts on the hills, with the golf ball marking the top of Lowther Hill.

The descent begins from the first mast, however if you decide to take a trip up to the view point at the 'golf ball' don't hang around too long or the 130MHz output might make you feel a bit warm-headed.

 The Enterkin Pass

Prepare to forget the previous two-thirds of this ride. From the outside of the corner beside the first mast, descend on the fast, wide gravel trail southwest until you reach the telephone poles.. The descent follows the telephone poles south down the steep sided valley south.

There is serious potential for speed here, only dampened by the tiny ribbon of singletrack that keeps you from rolling down into the bottom of the valley.

 Glen Valentine

The Enterkin Pass levels out after a couple of kilometres and traverses alongside the burn for another kilometre to where you reach a double track at the entrance to Glenvalentine (xxx). As the double track turns sharply left, follow the short, sharp climb south up into farmland.

The trail continues south on grassy terrain through gates and after a km you are faced with a peak directly in front of you. Traverse to the left of the peak and cross the barbed wire fence into the field, continuing to traverse around the hill, fighting the temptation to lose your height down the hillside to your left. Ride the ridge south through more gates until you reach the road.

 Tarmac Again

Hit the road at the signpost pointing back into the Enterkin Pass. From here it is a straight cruise down the road. Take care after 1km as you go straight over a hard-to-see crossroad. After a couple of kilometres the road bends sharply left and descends down to the A702. Turn right with care and follow the road downhill for a further few kilometres until you reach a right turn signposted for the castle. From here follow the road for another couple of kilometres over the main A76 with care and back into the long driveway to the Castle.

If you're back in time for the castle café – you've done well!

Summary

It's almost impossible to give a route description for this ride. There are so many twists and turns to it that you'll almost start to feel dizzy. Despite the length of the route, you never manage to get more than three kilometres away from the start. Cleverly though, you never feel like you're covering old ground as each new loop in the beautiful mature woodlands brings something fresh into the equation.

The setting for the riding is something else too. On entering the estate grounds you are directed straight up the pink gravel driveway towards Drumlanrig Castle, a most imposing vista, and then into the mature oak and beech woods of the Drumlanrig Estate. And with the final part of the ride up the same impressive driveway, the scenery is unusual to say the least. Not a ride you'll forget in a hurry.

There are also all mod cons here, with a state of the art environmentally friendly bike wash, showers and changing rooms, bike shop and hire, and a choice of cafes.

Drumlanrig

Expert

Hard

16 km

400 m

1.5 - 3 hrs

Landranger 78

Getting There

Drumlanrig is located between Thornhill and Sanquhar on the A76.

From the north - from the M74 take the A702 just south of Abington, towards Carronbridge. Look out for the signpost to Drumlanrig (right) just before entering Carronbridge.

From the south - from the M74, at Gretna take the A75 west to Dumfries. At Dumfries follow the ring road round and take the exit for Thornhill on the A76. Continue through Thornhill towards Sanquhar for 5 kilometres. Look out for Drumlanrig Castle signposted off left just after Carronbridge.

Start Point

From the road drive up the pink gavel driveway, pay your parking fee and park in the estate car park. All the bike routes start at the far end of the castle car park (opposite the entrance). Ride up the wide track to start until you see the signs for red and black routes.

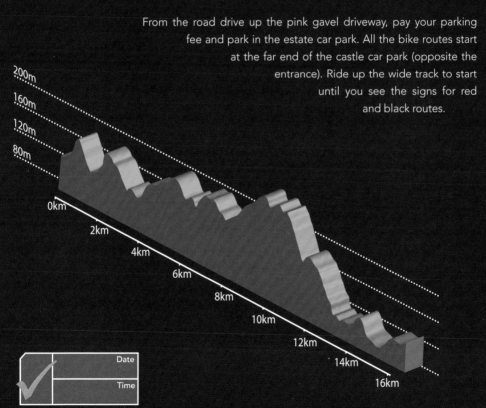

	Date	
✓	Time	

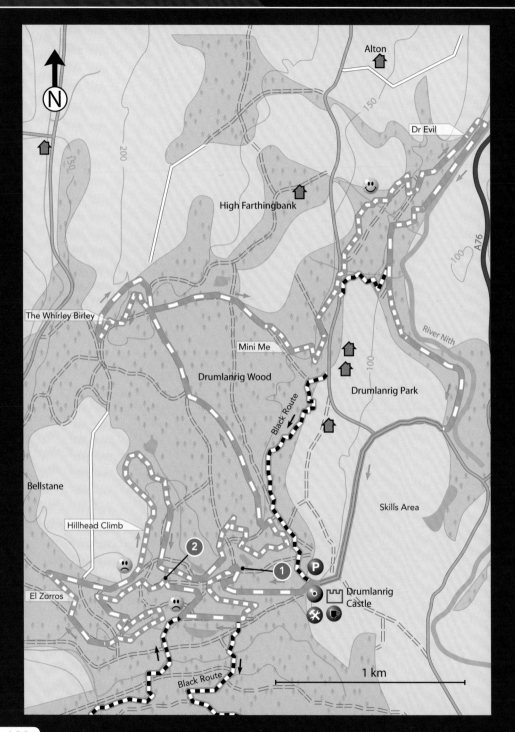

Route Description

1 Crossroads

A short ride uphill on the track takes you into the depths of the forest. At a crossroads, small markers with either a black or red border direct you towards the route. At the crossroads, dive into the woods for an introduction to the fast rooty trails that Drumlanrig specialises in. Pop out onto the track briefly and then fly back in for more twisting action.

Do this on a dry day and you'll glide over the roots, a bit of wetness and it all gets that wee bit more technical. And on really wet days, just don't hit those brakes or you'll be sliding all over the place.

2 Kiln Knowe Climb

Life continues on pleasantly, twisting and turning through the forest with plenty of tight turns around trees and short rooty drops to keep you on your toes. Eventually though, what goes down must go up and the short but sharp technical climb of Kiln Knowe helps you regain some lost altitude.

From here a fast tight traverse takes you to a short section of forest road and then alongside the edge of the woodland for the Hillhead Climb.

From here a series of short elegant singletrack sections on brown earthy lines interspersed with forest roads leads you almost back to where you started and the original crossroads.

3 Crossroads

For red riders, the trail now takes a long leisurely ride back through the forest on forest track, finishing off with a little wiggle along the 'Whirley Birley' singletrack to the corner of the fields. Then doubletrack along the edge of the woods before heading back into the woods and on to 'Mini Me' and a long delicious section of high-speed frolicks.

4 TT Climb

Doubletrack then takes you up to 'Dr Evil' and the penultimate laid-back amble alongside the river, passing signs for the black route at 'the TT Climb' as you go. If you want a harder finish, turn right here and go up the TT and follow black markers back to the trail end.

Other rides at Drumlanrig

The black trail offers a slightly harder version of the Red, with more tight singletrack, high speed ribbons of dirt and the hallmark rooty fun. There are endless options to combine the two trails to make your own perfect version of a ride.

As we know in the world of mtb trail building, nothing stands still for long, and Drumlanrig is no exception to this. Rik has endless plans to improve the courses here and over the next couple of years his aim is to practically eliminate all of the forest track sections from the trail. This will include around half a dozen kilometres of new track on both the black and the red courses and a skills loop out the front of the castle.

bikeraX

Dumfriesshire

Summary

Why the name? Well there's a cemetery at the start of the ride and another at the end, and lots of hills in between, what this means we're not sure but you have been warned!

Starting from lofty Wanlockhead, the highest village in Scotland sitting at 460m above sea level, this route is like a taster for riding in the Highlands – there's remote, featureless hills, tracks that bear little relation to the OS Map, sections of hike-a-bike, and even a burn crossing where you can get your feet wet. It pretty much ticks all the boxes for 'Highland Epic', except you're south of Glasgow, only 10 mins from the M74 and there's a café at the end, as long as it's still summertime when you finish.

The section named 'Dempster Road' on the map is a bit misleading – this sheep track is one of the narrowest, most excellent descents you'll find anywhere, as long as you can

Wanlockhead	
Expert	
3 with short sections of 4	
30 km	
1100 m	
3 - 5 hrs	
Landranger 78	

hold the line. Once you've tackled this 'Sheep-Track-Of-Certain-Doom' and forded the burn, it's down the road to the low-lying farms and the charmingly named 'Bogg', before returning along, up and down the Southern Upland Way.

It's definitely a fair weather ride, as these hill tracks become very wet after rain(!) and won't stand up to winter use (see the responsible access guidelines). As well as this the Visitor Centre at Wanlockhead is closed during the winter and you'll certainly want to pop in to the tea room for a coffee and a jacket potato when you've finished.

Getting There

Wanlockhead is on the B797 between Sanquhar and Elvanfoot, 8 miles from junction 14 on the M74. From the south leave the M74 at J14, from the North leave at J13, the Wanlockead Lead Mining Museum is well signposted from both exits.

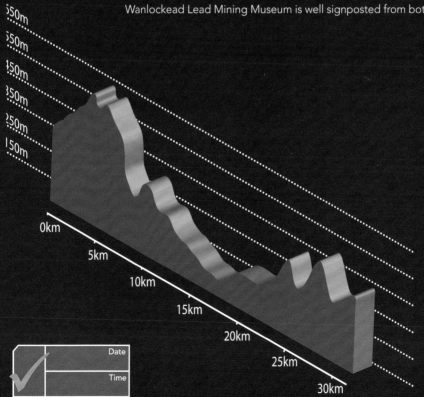

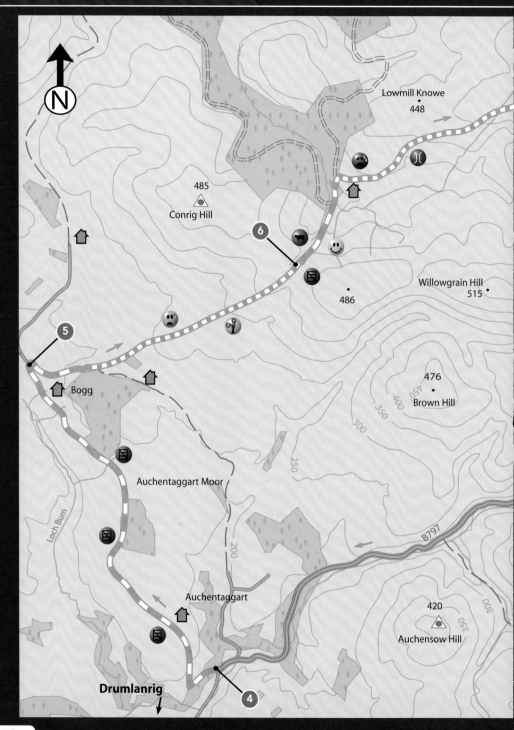

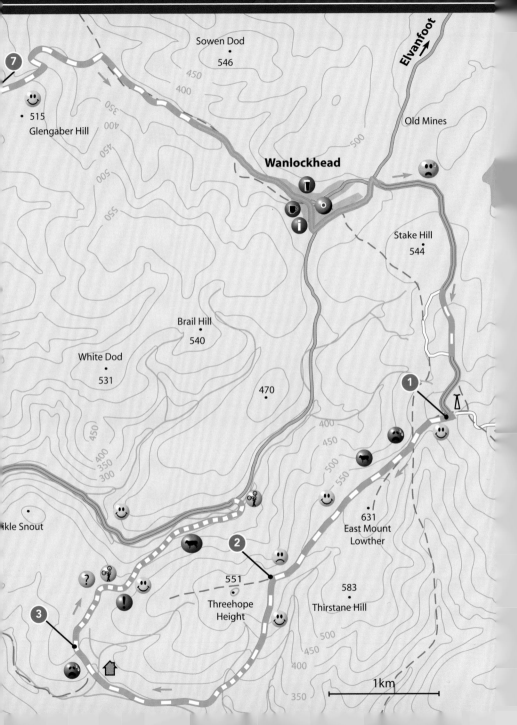

Elvanfoot

Sowen Dod
546

7

515
Glengaber Hill

Old Mines

Wanlockhead

Stake Hill
544

Brail Hill
540

White Dod
531

470

1

631
East Mount
Lowther

ikle Snout

2

551

Threehope
Height

583
Thirstane Hill

3

1km

Route Description

Start

From the Visitor Centre head up the hill to the main road and turn left passing the cemetery on your right. At the edge of the village take the right turn on the tarmac road up to the giant golf ball on the hill - the Lowther Complex Transmitter Station.

When you reach a fence on your left take the track across the wooden bridge and follow the fence line up hill, or you can stay on the road if you want to make it easier. You rejoin the tarmac after 1km and continue to climb to the mast.

1 The Mast

Follow the road as it bends around to the left under the mast then take the doubletrack which dives steeply down to the right following a fence line on the left. The gravel surface quickly turns to grass, heading swiftly down to a shoulder and then up the other side, less hastily.

Still climbing you come to a fork, go right on the easier route that contours around below the summit of East Mount Lowther. The grassy track soon starts descending, but before long you're pointing uphill again

2 Left fork

Go left at the fork in the track, still heading uphill for now, but the track soon starts loosing height very quickly. This is one of the steepest descents you'll ever do, so even die-hard XC racers might want to drop the saddle a bit for this.

Half way down the obvious grass track turns into vague singletrack, but as long as you

keep pointing downhill you shouldn't go too far wrong.

When you run out of downhill you hit a double track where you turn right and cross a small burn to soon join another grassy doubletrack. Bear right again here to take you onto an easy flat section of track. When the deserted farm at Glenim comes into view take the right fork, leading you uphill and around the back of the farm then bear right on the stone track which drops down before zigzagging up the hill in front of you to the stone sheepfold.

3 Sheepfold

Keep the sheepfold on your left and follow the grass track north. It soon bends to the right and starts heading uphill. Follow the line of shooting butts on your left until you reach number 7, then bear left for a short hike-a-bike section where no path seems to exist. Keep the shooting butts on you left and quite soon you should see the masts on Lowther Hill again and the road below you.

At butt number 2, turn right heading towards a scar of orange dirt on the hillside, if you're lucky you might pick up a vague path here. You should be able to make out the sheeptrack wonder of the Dempster Road heading down the side of the hill in front of you.

Make the sketchy crossing at the top of the gully to pick up the top of the track and follow this narrowest of lines down to the stone sheepfold at the bottom. Then get your feet wet crossing the burn and hike up to the road and head downhill for 6km

4 Farm Track

After crossing the river take the second turning on the right. This begins as a metalled

oad but soon turns to farm track. Follow it to
the farm at Auchentaggart and bear left at
the buildings and up through the first of eight
gates between here and Bogg.

5 Southern Upland Way

About 100m past the farm at Bogg, take a
sharp right, on a gentle gradient heading back
towards the conifer plantation that you just
passed. You're now following the Southern
Upland Way back to Wanlockhead.

As you reach the woodland take the
waymarked path on the left, leaving the track
behind. The stony path soon disappears, but
the waymarkers show the way to a stile, after
which the path is quite obvious, climbing
between two fence lines to another stile.

After a short open section and another stile
the path is again in a fence sandwich. After
the next stile the climb turns brutal - you'll
probably be pushing for the next 100m or so.
As you near the top the track becomes clearer
and you can enjoy a pleasant ride along the
top to a gate.

6 Gate

Straight on at the gate as you start descending
with a steep gully on your left. The track is
wide, grassy and fast. Check your watch, it's
nooning time! At the bottom go through the
gate and turn right on the forest track.

At the Southern Upland Way signpost turn
right on the doubletrack, leaving the forest
and heading back into the hills. Bear left
following the Southern Upland Way markers
before the buildings at Cogshead.

There's a long steady climb ahead of you so
feel free to reach for the granny ring. Halfway
up there's a couple of narrow bridges to cross

with a worrying drop to the right, then it's just
up to the top.

7 The Top

Go through the gate at the top and get ready
to lose all that height you've just earned. The
grassy doubletrack is a bit washed out in
places, but is potentially a very fast descent.
This route is popular with walkers though, so
be aware of that as you drop down to Wanlock
Water.

Cross the bridge at the bottom and turn right
on the track, head past the cemetery and back
up to Wanlockhead for tea and scones.

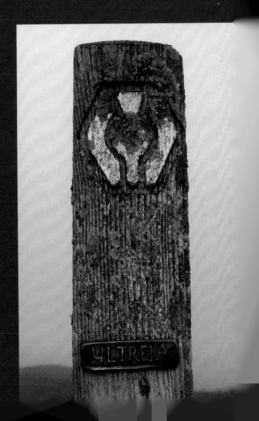

Summary

A mixture of classic Scottish moorland scenery, patchwork heathery hillsides, remote bothies and daft grouse make for an off beat ride to unwind on. There's no real technical difficulty as most of the riding is on wide paths and tracks. The challenge, if you want one, is to ride all the way up the stony track to the top of Glenleith Fell clean and then to see how fast you dare go on the way down the other side. And the bonus is that the harsh but fair hill gets 90% of the climbing out of the way early on.

Glenleith Fell is a ride best done on a hardtail and a fine day, when the simple pleasures of a fast blast down never-ending moorland tracks, are something to relish. Navigation and conditions can both be pretty harsh up on the fell when the weather is bad, so pack a map and compass just in case the cloud comes down.

Durisdeer	
Classic	
Moderate	
32 km	
950 m	
2.5 - 4 hrs	
Landranger 78	

Getting There

From the M74

Head off the motorway at junction 14 towards Elvanfoot. Continue through Elvanfoot, heading south on the A702. At Durisdeermill turn left to Durisdeer and follow the narrow road up and through the ford to a junction in the village. Turn left at the junction and park by the church.

From Thornhill and Dumfries

From Thornhill go north along the A76 to Carronbridge. At Carronbridge turn right up the A702 towards Elvanfoot. At Durisdeermill turn left to Durisdeer.

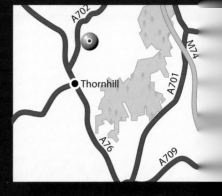

Start Point

Park in front of the church at Durisdeer, being very careful to leave plenty of room for access.

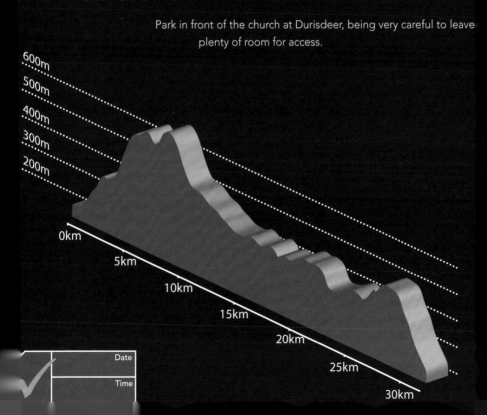

600m
500m
400m
300m
200m

0km
5km
10km
15km
20km
25km
30km

Date

Time

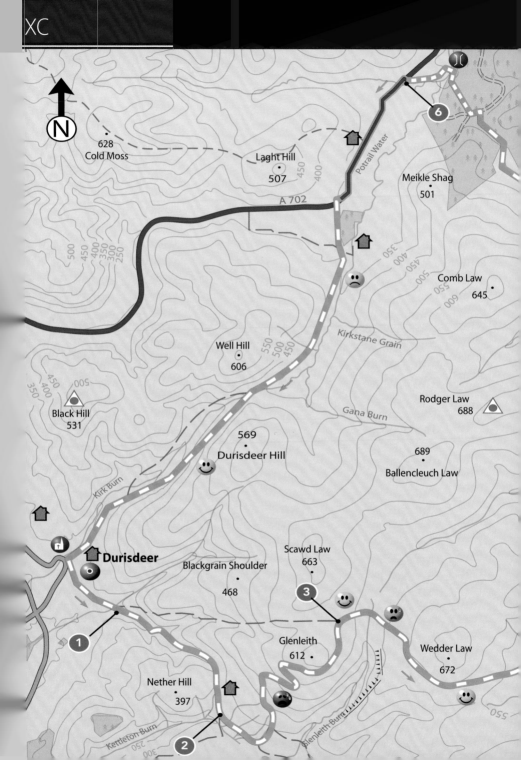

N

628
Cold Moss

Laght Hill
507

A 702

Potrail Water

6

Meikle Shag
501

Comb Law
645

Kirkstane Grain

Well Hill
606

Gana Burn

Rodger Law
688

Black Hill
531

569
Durisdeer Hill

689
Ballencleuch Law

Kirk Burn

Durisdeer

Blackgrain Shoulder

468

Scawd Law
663

3

1

Glenleith
612

Wedder Law
672

Nether Hill
397

Kettleton Burn

2

Glenleith Burn

Route Description

1 Fork in track

At a fork in the track, a smooth steep Land Rover track goes off leftwards. Stay on the main trail up the centre of the gorge until you come to a gate and a ruined cottage at the top. This part of the track is loose and steep in parts. Go through the gate and continue more easily along the track to another building.

2 Building

At the buildings take the left branch of the track and continue to a fork. At the fork go leftwards and double back on yourself (good views here of the gorge you have just ridden up).

The track starts off easily enough, but you know there's got to be some pain to come as the hill rises up in front of you. As the track steepens up and the surface gets more stony, you'll need to dig deep to carry on riding. Just as long as you keep enough speed to keep the front wheel going in a straight line, you can make it to the top.

Finally the track levels off and you can look up and enjoy the outstanding moorland scenery of the Lowther Hills. This compact group of hills has a real Highland feel to it.

3 Junction

At a junction with a new pink track that is not marked on the OS map go right and start descending. This is the track which broke off left at WP1, and can be used as a fast descent if all you fancy is a quick blast up Glenleith Fell.

A fast descent now takes you down to Glenleith Burn. The brief respite from climbing ends sadly at the burn and the hut as one last section of ascent rears up in front of you. Pop it back into the granny gear for a pithy little re-ascent up onto Wedder Law.

Once the Wedder Law ascent is out of the way the trail meanders onwards towards Daer Reservoir going down and down and down forever. At last some payback for all that ascending. Ride it as fast as you like, only a couple of gates need watching out for here and there. At the bottom of the valley, cross a couple of makeshift bridges and go through Kirkhope Farm and onto tarmac.

④ Kirkhope Farm

Once on the tarmac, follow the road around the side of the reservoir heading into the forest as you pass the dam wall. About 700m after the dam wall, a forest track goes off left. The track is signposted 'Southern Upland Way'.

⑤ Southern Upland Way

The trail now follows The Southern Upland Way for the next five kilometres. At first the trail follows forest roads, then crosses moorland to another block of forestry. Here the SUW heads off the forest tracks and turns into a good hard packed path, giving excellent straightforward riding.

As the path exits the forest it becomes a little vague and boggy. Follow the trail over a narrow bridge and a couple of stiles to the main road.

⑥ Main road

Turn left on the road and continue for 2 kilometres to a stand of trees on the left. Take the track going down the right hand side of the forest. Follow this down to a gate and then continue rightwards along the track towards a col in the distance.

A short ascent takes you up to the start of the final descent. The track drops steeply from the col and back to Durisdeer to give a very fine end to the day's riding.

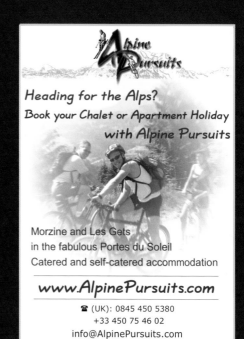

Summary

As a longstanding DH venue on the National Point Series circuit, the tracks at Ae have been raced on by all the names and greats in downhill history over the years. The track is now a real tight mixture of old school and new, with plenty of well worn in natural lines, built up jumps and natural stepdowns off rocks and roots.

Tight singletrack through trees, gap jumps and the 'piece de resistance', a massive hucking drop to finish. If all that doesn't get you salivating, and throwing the bike in the car straight away, then get rid of your full face helmet now. This track is a real pleasure to ride.

Ae	
Downhill	DH
5 with the Drop Off at the end	4
2.2 km	
220m	
3 mins +	
Landranger 78	

Getting There

According to the 7stanes leaflet Ae is just 19 minutes from Junction 16 of the M74, but it's very easy to get lost in the maze of minor roads. If you've got satnav the postcode is DG1 1.

From the motorway

After exiting the motorway at Johnstonebridge, take the minor road towards the A701 and St Annes. Turn left onto the A701 and follow to the bridge at Ae Bridgend. Go right to Ae village and then turn right again into the forest. Go through the FC complex and bear round to the right over 2 cattlegrids and into the car park on the left.

From Dumfries

Take the A701 road north signposted Moffat. After Amisfield Town, turn left onto the road signposted Ae and Forest of Ae. The trail head is located just after Ae village.

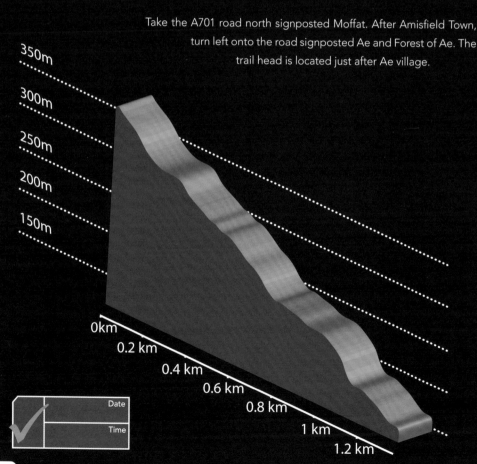

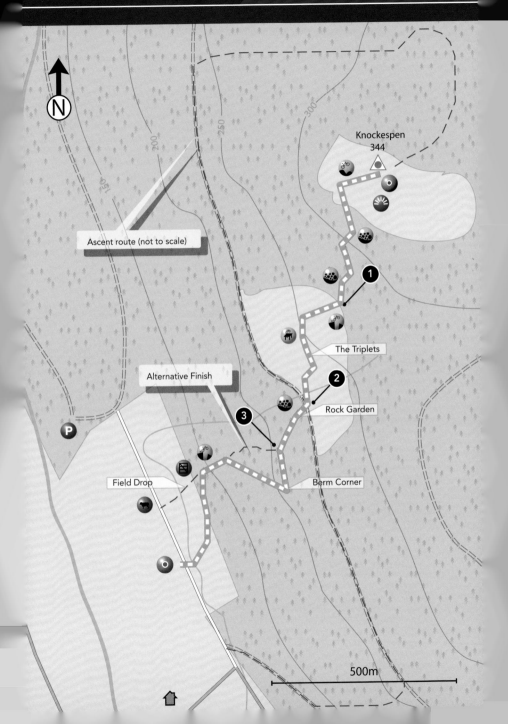

Knockespen
344

Ascent route (not to scale)

1

The Triplets

Alternative Finish

2

Rock Garden

3

P

Field Drop

Berm Corner

500m

N

Getting to the start

1. The quick way up

Head out of the car park and head back down the road towards the forestry offices. After the second cattle grid turn left to follow a path up to the massive drop at the end of the trail. From here, it's pretty steep but you can push up the track, mostly on little trails off to the side, but beware of riders coming down.

'DONT TRY THIS AT WEEKENDS'

2. The official way up

It's a long old haul to the top along the fire roads, but at least it's an easy one to have to do on a full bounce rig. Go back to the right turn to the FC offices and go straight on taking the forest track on the left. At the first junction go left, follow the track past the DH course at the Rock Garden and then go left at the next junction and then right and right again to arrive at the top of the hill next to the Trig Point.

3. The best way of all.

Use the Uplift Service. Just at the time of writing (summer 2006) the Forestry Commission Scotland has suspended the uplift service because of Health and Safety legislation. Watch the 7stanes website for news of this Tally's AeUp service and its reinstatement.

DH ## Route description

From the top of Knockespen Hill, a steep start takes you down a wide rock strewn hillside with a choice of lines. Choose a complicated rock garden at the start on the right or a jump at the bottom on the left. From the jump, keep some speed through the flat and then steeply down through the rutted slope to a choke at the bottom. Choice of lines here, old school narrow and rutted on the right, or stay left for some loose rocky stuff with the odd short drop.

After the choke, kick round to the left for an off camber traverse along the hillside with small drops and natural step downs leading into the trees and a sharp righthander. Bend round to the right and tight earthy singletrack snakes through small trees followed by a loose ball bearings section taking the fall line then leading left to a straight with loads of small natural jumps.

① Gap Jump

As you come out of the trees, gap jump over a stream on the left or chicken run on the right. Track goes across the open hillside, lefthand berm, jump, tabletop, the Triplets and a series of doubles leading into a tight steep chicane with a huge tree stump in the middle of it. Right takes you over a drop or left down the rut followed by a jump right or steep exit left onto the fire road.

② Rock Garden

Four lines face you on the down side of the fire road. A very sorry chicken run on the right avoids all the fun altogether. The next line left takes you through the big rock garden. Left again for a straightforward line down a rocky patio and to the far left a big drop in with a good landing followed by a jump.

Go back into the trees with a run of jumps and parallel lines giving plenty of options.

③ Split in trail

At this point an old line heads off rightwards giving you a choice of finishes.

Line 1

Stay on the main track, traverse the hill leftwards with a ski ramp and a gap jump on the left, or bypass this staying on the main track. Tight switchback with a high steep berm goes right.

Keep your speed out of the berm and down a steep rooty section with a choice of lines taking you down to the monster Stepdown at the bottom. Check out the drop before you ride it (2 step chicken run on the left), landing past the log with a good run out into a big berm. Berms and jumps take you to a finish at a gate and through this the infamous 'Field Drop'.

Line 2

Tight earthy singletrack sweeps left through the trees, narrowing to wheel wide ruts, sharp rooty switchbacks which you might want to jump, and a steep finish down to the monster drop.

Several other lines heading down off this track as you traverse across. At the drop a nice ramp takes you down the right hand side and drops you into the berms. Head left and nail it to the bottom.

And as if this isn't enough you can combine a couple of runs here with a session getting plenty of air on the 'Omega Man'.

Other routes at Ae

Of course the DH isn't the only good riding at Ae. The Omega Man is worth pushing up for. You can get to this by going a little further out on the DH ascent. The Omega Man gives you nearly three kilometres of jumps which encourage lift off big style. Be careful of the drop-offs – they may take you by surprise.

Just recently opened and by all account still a work in progress, the Ae Line Scottish Power Renewables Trail, as it is so concisely titled, is a 20 km cross country trail built with fun in mind and graded Red. A late addition to the 7stanes stable of routes and one of many parts, this route will definitely keep you on your toes. It's got all the things that XC riders love, including the hideous uphill of 'Nil Desperandum', tight technical singletrack, strange and sudden rock gardens and quite schizophrenic jumps as well as a bit of 'lite freeride' on the Omega Man.

To get to the route, follow the track out of the car park alongside the river and then follow waymarkers. Allow 2 – 4 hours for the ride.

A half day here also combines well with a quick pop across to the other side of the A702 for a half day on dirt at Drumlanrig Castle. The advantage of doing this in the afternoon is that you can then wash your bike, visit Rik at the Bike Shed, and eat tea and buns in the Castle café.

More routes

As well as Ae Forest, Dumfriesshire is also host to two further 7stanes centres, Mabie Forest and Dalbeattie. Both forests have plenty of quality riding that adds to the total variety that the 7stanes has to offer.

Mabie

Mabie forest lies just 4 miles from Dumfries on the A710 Solway Coast road. To get there, pass through the village of Islesteps and the entrance to the Forest is soon reached on the right hand side of the road.

Facilities

The trail head has parking, toilets, bike wash and a bike shop. The shop, which also does repair and hire, is run by G & G cycles. Their main shop is in Dumfries, but they keep plenty of stock here too. There's currently a small fledgling café but G&G are looking to expanding this too.

Trails

There are two well known trails here; the Endura Phoenix Trail, 17km of swooping singletrack graded red, and the Kona Dark Side, a 2km raised timber trail AKA 'North Shore', graded double black. As well as these, there is a newer section of timber trail, known locally as 'The Qualifier'. Do this piece of North Shore first and you may just 'qualify' for the real thing.

As well as these there are also plenty of gentle cycling options, such as the 11km Woodhead Loop which takes you through beautiful woodland on wide forest tracks and simple singletrack.

Mabie is another one of those forests that takes a while to get to know. If you want to shortcut the wandering about trying to find the good variations, you need to talk to a few locals.

Try popping in to see Clive down the road at the Criffel Inn, and he might just give you the lowdown on his own 'Alternative Red'. Clive's version takes you in from the village of New Abbey, adds some good extra distance to the Phoenix Trail and pops onto sections of the Kona Dark Side for extra value. For more information, you'll just have to buy Clive a pint.

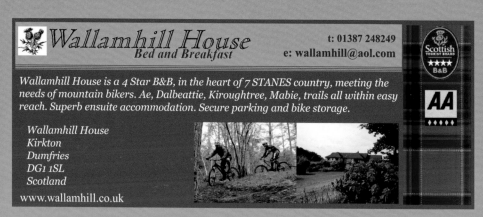

Dalbeattie

Just down the road from Mabie Forest is Dalbeattie, home of The Hardrock Trail and infamous Dalbeattie granite slabs.

To get here, head south west out of Dumfries on the A711 to Dalbeattie and then take the A710 south to Dalbeattie Forest.

At Dalbeattie town centre the trail head at the Richorn car park is just 150 metres from the end of the town's main road (just past where the high street joins the A710), on the left hand side.

Trails

Without doubt the best known of all the routes here, the Hardrock Trail 'rocks', as they say in the 7stanes. Littered with boulder pavements, wee granite slabs followed by monster granite slabs and the usual liberal smattering of very sweet singletrack, the Hardrock is another classic tick on the 7stanes circuit.

All around the trail, there are loads of clever little options to mix up the trail as hard or as easy as you like.

Also in the forest is the family friendly 10km Ironhash Trail and the 14km blue graded Moyle Hill Trail, both of which enjoy quiet corners of forest on wide trails and easy singletrack.

Facilities

As facilities go there's not a lot at the car park at the moment, though plans are in the offing to get at least a toilet block here. Cafes, pubs and shops are all to be found in Dalbeattie, just down the road.

Galloway

22

Newton Stewart

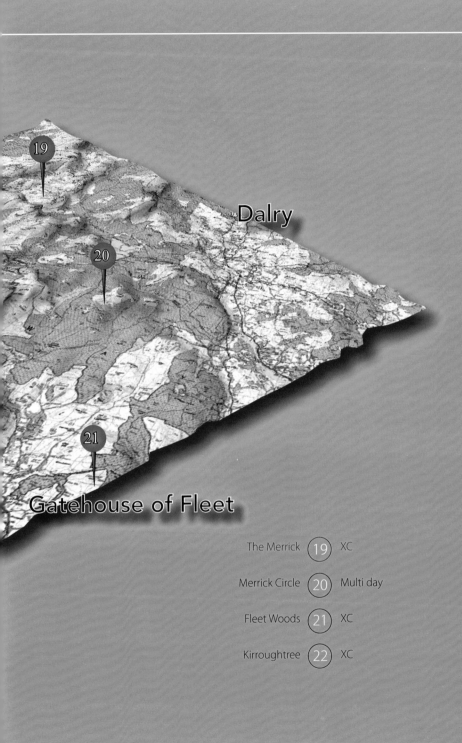

Dalry

Gatehouse of Fleet

The Merrick (19) XC

Merrick Circle (20) Multi day

Fleet Woods (21) XC

Kirroughtree (22) XC

Introduction

Many call this area a mini Highlands, and it is certainly true that for just that extra hours driving west from the motorway, you could be in a smaller version of the Scottish Highlands, with mountain and moor, coast and forest and wide open spaces.

The area boasts two of the 7stanes trail centres, Kirroughtree and Glentrool and both are very different in nature to each other. Choose from the gentle forest trails of Glentrool to the rocky, bermed and unabashed technicality of Kirroughtree.

As well as this, the highest mountain in the area, the Merrick, provides a wicked old school technical descent, which in the 'old school way' has to be earned first with a bit a bit of pushing and shoving to get to the top.

You won't find quite so many other mountain bike riders in this part of the world and this is part of the charm. Indeed in many remote corners of the region you are more likely to see a deer or a bird of prey than another human being. The Galloway hills provide plenty of space for exploring and multi day trips, with the mellow Solway coastline offering opportunities for plenty of gentle rides with the family.

Getting there

From the North - From Glasgow take the A77 to Ayr and then continue on to Girvan and pick up the A714 for Glentrool or take the A713 for New Galloway and Kirroughtree.

From the South - Just after Carlisle on the M74 head west for Dumfries. Stay on the A75 around Dumfries and continue on westwards. For Kirroughtree turn off the A75 at Palnure or continue on to Glentrool on the Girvan Road A714 from Newton Stewart.

Accommodation

Galloway has just about every sort of accommodation you could imagine, from the usual hotel and B&B to rather more unusual forms of lodgings at lighthouses and wigwams.

The very comfortable Murray Arms, www.murrayarms.com, at Gatehouse of Fleet has a secure bike store and bike wash and makes a good base for exploring this part of the world.

Rowallan House www.rowallan.co.uk, in Newton Stewart, and the Stables Guest House, www.stablesguesthouse.com, both have a lock up and bike wash.

For self catering Rusko Holidays www.ruskoholidays.co.uk , at Gatehouse of Fleet offer secluded cottages in a very scenic setting, and Killantre Cottages offer stylish self catering at New Port William near Newton Stewart (www.killantraecottages.com).

Food & Drink

Kirroughtree Visitor Centre has a friendly café which is open 10 – 5pm through May to Sept and weekends only through the winter

Glentrool/Galloway Forest Park Visitor Centre also has a nice little café. Open 10 – 5pm from mid April to the end of October.

For an after ride treat of organic ice, cream visit the Cream o Galloway at Rainton, just outside Gatehouse of Fleet. The Murray Arms do all day food and just around the corner The Masonic Arms has an award winning menu.

Bike shops and hire

Castle Douglas Cycle Centre is your best bet of any bike needs and is located just off the High Street on Church Street, Castle Douglas. They do a friendly repair and service deal as well as offer a host of spares and retail opportunities.

More info

Tourist Information Centres

Gatehouse of Fleet: on the High Street, 01557 814212.

Newton Stewart, 01671 402431.

www.scotlandwhisky.com

www.visitdumfriesandgalloway.co.uk/cycling

www.visitsouthwestscotland.com

www.gallowaycycling.co.uk

The Murray Arms Hotel

Gatehouse of Fleet

ALL DAY FOOD
Open All Year

We offer the following facilities:-

*   Secure Storage for Bikes
*   Washing Facilities for Bikes
*   Workstand
*   Drying Facilities
*   Washing Facilities
*   Packed Lunches
*   Good Food - available all day
*   Comfortable, En Suite Rooms
*   Warm, Friendly Welcome

Ideally Situated to Tour the 7 Stanes
Just 20 minutes from Mabie, Dalbiettie
and Kirroughtree mtb centres

New breakfast, brunch, lunch & dinner
menus
Top quality food, sourced locally

For Further Information or to make a Booking,
please call in or telephone us
Phone – 01557 814 207
www.murrayarmshotel.co.uk
email – info@murrayarmshotel.co.uk

"We look forward to welcoming you"

Summary

Narrow singletrack, open moorland, fast flying descents, forest, mountain and moorland; the ride up and down the Merrick ticks just about every box going. The descent down Merrick offers superb technical riding and is one of the finest natural descents going in the whole of Southern Scotland. Like all natural downhill courses though, the ride down has to be earned first with a bit of pushing and shoving and a long arduous route to the top.

Don't be put off though, this is an out and out adventurer's ride, and what you get out is exactly equivalent to what goes in. The riding is varied all the way and highly technical in places. You may only find yourself riding about half of it on the way up, but you'll be loath to get out of your saddle on the way down, it's that much fun.

Glentrool	
Expert	
Extreme	4
13 km	
887 m	
3 - 5 hrs	
Explorer 318	

Getting There

The ride starts in the Glentrool forest park at the Buchan monument.

To get there, turn off the A75 at Newton Stewart onto the A714 heading north towards Girvan. At Bargrennan turn right to Glentrool village. In the village go right again to Stroan Bridge. This is the Glentrool Forest Park Visitor Centre with toilets and tearooms, also the start of the 'ungradeable' 58km Glentrool ride.

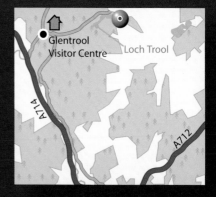

Carry on up the lane, passing Glentrool Lodge, and parking in an obvious parking area just before the end of the road and the Buchan Monument.

Start Point

At the end of the road, just as the lane bends round to the right and starts to descend, a narrow grey path heads upwards. Ride up this until stopped by the boulder chokes just before the fence. An odd bit of carrying around the bigger steps (unless you're a trials riding fanatic) and you reach the fence and gate.

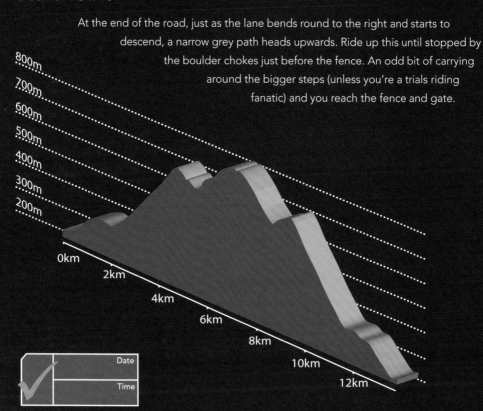

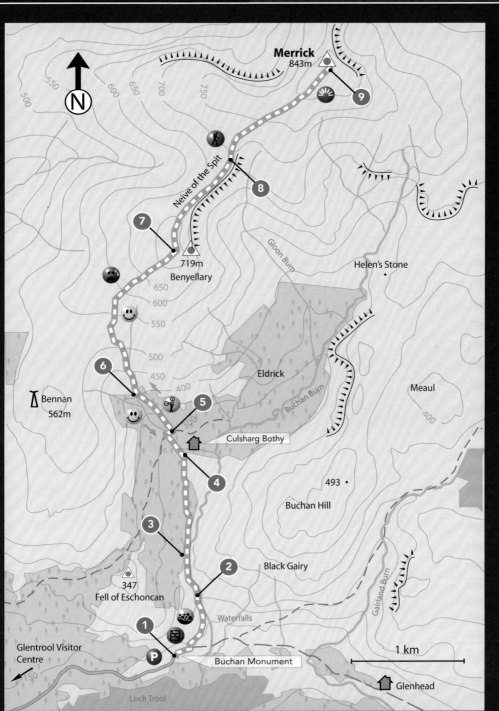

N

Merrick
843m

9

Neive of the Spit

8

7

719m
Benyellary

Gloon Burn

Helen's Stone

Eldrick

Buchan Burn

Meaul

6

5

Bennan
562m

Culsharg Bothy

4

493
Buchan Hill

3

2

Black Gairy

347
Fell of Eschoncan

Waterfalls

Gairland Burn

1 km

1

Glentrool Visitor
Centre

P

Buchan Monument

Glenhead

Loch Trool

Route Description

Just a quick word of caution on this route. The Merrick is a high mountain and can be very exposed to weather from the west, so go prepared and better still wait for one of those fine dry summer days, when the views, the riding and the company are all just perfect. Allow 2.5 hours for the ascent and 1 hour for the descent.

1 Gate

At the gate the path veers steeply up to the left. No matter how good your riding is, this is a definite hike a bike section. Shoulder your bike and make your way upwards. Thankfully it's only a short section and then you're back on your bike dodging boulders again.

2 Back in the saddle

At the top of the short rise, the path levels out, running alongside the forest. Like the bit before the gate, ride it in sections – some of it is straightforward, other parts require the balance and strength of a Bolshoi ballet dancer.

3 Forest Edge

As you enter the forest, the path widens, and although it starts off a bit damp and tricky, soon dries and eases and turns into a flowing ribbon of well surfaced trail.

The trail descends slightly and speedily until you end up at a small clearing next to a stream and an old house, the Cusharg Bothy.

4 Old House

Carry on up the path on the left hand side of the house with some more climbing up to a forest track.

5 Forest Track

Cross the track and continue up the stony path on the other side. Depends how big your thighs are, but most likely you'll be walking a fair amount of this. Just grit your teeth and think of the descent…

6 Top of forest / Grey path

Finally exit the forest and rest a few minutes to get your breath back. From here it's rideable just about all the way to the summit. Take the well surfaced path up the open moorland towards the top of Benyellary at 719m.

The hardest obstacle here is hopping the drainage culverts. They must expect a lot of rain here, as in some places they're a foot deep and a foot wide. Usually a well propelled bounce with a bit of rolling speed gets you over them.

7 Benyellary 719m

With most of the climbing and hard work done, it's well worth taking time out at this first summit to finally look around. From here you can see the path snaking along the ridge to the saddle of Nieve of the Spit and on up to the summit of Merrick.

Leave the summit of Benyellary and enjoy the brief descent to the saddle.

8 Saddle – Nieve of the Spit

The ascent isn't quite over yet, having lost some height, this has to be regained, but it's still just under 200 metres of ascent to the summit of Merrick. Straightforward grassy paths now take you slowly upwards to finally reach the top.

The Merrick 843m

The trig point and the summit come as a welcome break from peddling, and the summit shelter a welcome break from the insistent breeze. The views are superb and from here you have the chance to eye up the descent. A faint trail also disappears onwards along the ridge to later drop down to Loch Enoch in the east. By all accounts this is rideable, but we haven't been there yet, so if you go exploring you're on your own. Otherwise relax a while

The Descent

The descent is by exactly the same route you have just come up and is a full on blast. The way down starts off fast and grassy on the flanks of Merrick until you reach the saddle between the two peaks again. Then you have to make the short but very easy ascent back up to Benyellary.

The way off Benyallery is a little steeper and full of surprise and well hidden holes in the grass. Keep your wits about you as it looks innocent enough but can easily have you pogoing suddenly over the handlebars.

Pick up the surfaced path and weave rapidly down this. Luckily the culverts are much less of an obstacle on the way down and the front wheel easily rolls over them or with that little extra lift from gravity, jumped. Stopping quickly though, is not an option on the loose surface, so look out for walkers coming up the hill and control your speed.

At the edge of the forest, remember that painful push straight up and now get ready to enjoy descending it. This is pure fun, steep and fast, with loads of small natural obstacles to keep you on the ball.

Back at the forest track, cross over and head past the house, keeping some speed on for the slight rise into the forest. Go easily through the forest and look forward to the last trials style section of the trail.

The path narrows as you come out of the forest and is littered with random boulders, some passable some not. Have fun working out which ones are and which ones are not. At the end of this section is the short steep descent to the gate. Decide for yourself whether to ride it, but body armour might not be a bad idea for this.

After the gate, it's a mix of narrow trail, boulder chokes and short slabs back to the road. Enjoy them all. There's generally a soft landing in the heather on the side if you get it wrong, so you might as well give it a go. You'll have fun and some hilarious moments trying.

Once on the road, follow the sign to the monument and pick up the small trail heading downwards parallel to the road. With the odd slab and step, it's nice way to finish.

Summary

There's nothing like the adventure of heading out into the hills for a couple of days of peace and quiet and self sufficiency. With the aid of a bike trailer, a good mate and a bottle of something for the bothy, a simple adventure is easy to find in Galloway. Here the hills are both wild and remote, but none too steep, and with plenty of good Land Rover tracks to ease your passage and well kept bothies to provide shelter, all the ingredients are right for a memorable trip.

The Merrick Circle always keeps one eye on the ever present bulk of Merrick itself, but don't worry, it doesn't involve any of the killer climbs involved in an ascent of the mountain itself. Instead The Circle opts to explore the rolling landscape and numerous lochs surrounding the mountain and firmly keeps its feet firmly planted in the valleys and what ascents there are, are short and generally gentle.

Galloway

Rowantree Memorial
GR 353 096

Adventure

Moderate

85 km

1718 m

7 - 10 hrs

Explorer 318

Getting There

In theory you could start this ride more or less anywhere, but to get the bothy just about slap bang in the middle of the trip, and a café conveniently located about half way through each day, then the best starting point is the small car park at the Rowantree Memorial just north of Glentrool Visitor Centre.

To get there from the south -

Take the A75 to Newton Stewart. At the Newton Stewart roundabout, take the A714 to take you through the town and towards Girvan. As the road bends right over the river at Bargrennan, a small fork in the road signs you off right to Glentrool village and just beyond this, Glentrool Visitor Centre (signposted to Galloway Forest Park).

To get there from the north -

From Ayr, take the A77 to Maybole. As you go through Maybole, take the B7023 to the village of Crosshill. At Crosshill go straight on at the junction and take the minor road signposted - Cycle Route 7. Follow the narrow road to the small car park at the Rowantree Memorial.

Date	
Time	

N

Loch Doon

14

P

523
Craiglee

13

12

11

Backhill of
Bush

400
350

300
500

Craigmawhannal
357

Mullwharchar
662

P

Loch
Riecawr

Loch
Macaterick

400

GALLOWAY
FOREST PARK

Merrick
843

700

600

Loch
Bradan

Shiel Hill
505

15

Stinchar Bridge

16

500

600

4

Rowantree Memorial

P

Cairnfore Hill
248

269
Suie Hill

3

Craiglaigh Hill
401

1

Knapps
314

Bencallen
346

17

2

Bracklach Hill
263

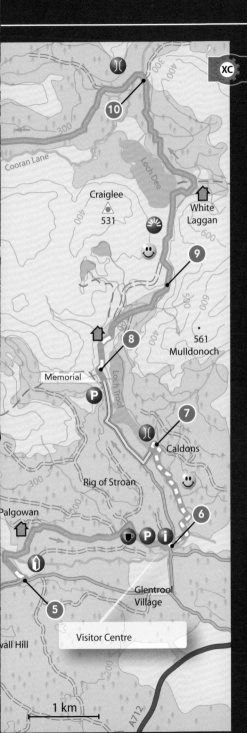

Route Description

Day 1

Rowantree Memorial to Blackhill of Bush Bothy

Distance 45km; Ascent 909m; Time 3.5 – 5 hrs

From the memorial car park, head back down the road to the fork. Go straight on for 1 kilometre to the first forest track on the right. Take this, climbing a little to start with and passing a small quarry, to arrive at a track junction.

1 Track Junction

Go left (as if doubling back on yourself) and follow this down for a quite a long way to another T junction overlooking Loch Moan. Go right here and then onwards for another 1.5km to another junction.

2 T Junction

Go left and then left again at another junction after 400m. Continue to a large junction where the track enters a broad fire break. Though the area around the fire break is now largely felled, you can still make out its old borders.

3 T junction

Go left and go downhill with wide sweeping views of Glentrool and the Merrick. At the bottom of this track you meet up with the road again.

4 Road

Go right and follow the road for 3 km. At the edge of some open fields is a track bearing left to Palgowan Bridge. The track is also marked with a green mtb sign.

 Road / Track

Turn left to Palgowan Bridge. After crossing the bridge, go rightwards, through a gate and back into the forest. Keep following the cycle trail signs (you are following the trail backwards at this point) to finally find yourself on the road just 100m away from the Glentrool Visitor Centre. Turn right to reach the Centre.

6 **Visitor Centre / Café**

The café marks the half way point on day one and is an excellent rest spot before the trail gets a bit rougher, then to be followed with an ascent to the bothy. From the Visitor Centre, follow the signs for the Southern Upland Way. The 'Way', as its known, is heralded by an ornate metal sign to the left of the bridge. Follow the path along pleasant singletrack along the edge of the Waters of Trool to a set of wooden footbridges. Carry / haul your

bikes and trailers across the bridge and go up the path to a signboard and turn left. Enjoy an easy fun section of singletrack with the odd sharp rise as far as Caldons campsite.

 Caldons Campsite

At Caldons 'The Way' has been diverted to repair some of the damage caused by erosion, both human and natural. Bikes are no longer allowed on this section, so turn left over a bridge and join the road. Turn right at the junction and go uphill on tarmac to the Memorial car park.

8 **Memorial car park**

At the end of the road, as the road turns into track, follow it round to the right (Cycle Route 7 markers).

The next section of trail takes you down a pleasant stony track through mature leafy woods. Shortly after a bridge the route diverts right (signed Cycle Route 7) along a path towards the river. At the river, go across the

bridge and follow the trail leftwards.

When you exit the path onto a forest track, go right and stay on this all the way to the top and the forest edge. A bit of hard work as the trail inches its way upwards is more than rewarded by the fantastic Glen views at the top of the forest.

 Edge of Forest

Go through the gate and follow the track upwards to the head of the glen. At the top, the view suddenly opens up in front of you with Loch Dee in the valley and the hills of the Rhinns of Kells in the backdrop. Relax and enjoy, as the trail drops down to the head of the loch.

Looking up rightwards from the stream at the head of the loch, you can just make out the small building that is the White Laggan Bothy.

From here, continue along the track as far as a T junction with a circular sheep pen on your left. Go left here and down to a bridge.

 Bridge

Turn left at the junction just past the bridge, and continue for approximately one kilometre to another track junction. Go left and head up the track through a large felled section until eventually you glimpse a white cottage in the distance.

This is the Blackhill of Bush Bothy and a comfortable and by now well earned rest for the night.

 Bothy

The little two room bothy is usually well stocked with wood for the wood burning stove, and being a little of the beaten track is generally clean and quiet. There are even some simple bunk beds to sleep on.

The Mountain Bothies Association (MBA) who maintain these simple shelters, simply ask that you leave the hut as you find it, and even a little bit better in some cases. And don't forget, everything you take in with you, you have to take back out.

Day 2

Blackhill of Bush to Rowantree Memorial

Distance 40km; Ascent 809m; Time 4 – 5 hrs

From the bothy, go left and continue along the track you came in on. Go straight on at a large track junction with a track heading off right. Stay on the track for about 5 km until just 500 m before it ends at the forest edge.

 Muddy quad track

Just as you round the last bend before the edge of the forest, you will see a muddy quad track heading downhill on the left. Unfortunately in wet weather this short unavoidable linking section can turn into a real mudfest.

Follow the track down to a flat bridge over the stream. Just stay with the line of the quad tracks, even when they appear to be going in the wrong direction. The track does a big S shape and after about half an hour of riding or pushing, depending on the weather, you arrive on a good (dry) track.

 Forest Track

Turn right and enjoy being on a hard surface again. Continue along here to a junction overlooking Loch Doon. Turn left, go over a bridge and keep going until you see a bigger bridge and the spectacular rocky slabs where the main river enters the loch. Go over the bridge and up to the Forest Drive. Turn right and ride alongside the lake to the little café at Craigmalloch Toll.

 Café

The little café used to be a cowshed, now it's a cosy rest and an opportunity to replenish before the last quarter of the ride.

After refreshments head back down the Forest Drive and stay on the easy hardpacked track all the way to Loch Bradan, passing on your way, what has to be the most far flung children's playground in Scotland!

After a slight hill passing Ballochbeatties Cottage with the wood carvings and old tree roots outside, meet the head of a minor road signposted to Stinchar Bridge.

 Road Head to Stinchar Bridge

Turn left and follow the road to Stinchar Bridge. If you've got the energy, some nice singletrack about half way along on the left, takes you on a little diversion via Crawberry Rock.

At Stinchar Bridge cross the road and go down old double track following some old blue waymarkers towards the Stinchar Falls. Follow the doubletrack to arrive on a forest track by a concrete bridge.

 Forest Track / Bridge

Go left and follow the forest track. Go right at the first junction (old blue markers hiding beside the trees). Follow the forest track as it goes high and then contours around the hillside high above the River Stinchar. Part way along, a nice little trail takes you down to the actual Stinchar Falls and then onto North Balloch.

However it does involve a big climb back out and no doubt by now you are just thinking of the homeward leg. So it's best to miss out a visit to the falls for now and keep contouring round the hillside until you meet up with the road.

 Road / Nick of the Balloch

As you leave the track, the end is now truly in sight. Turn left and climb up through the Nick of the Balloch pass and then pick up speed as you come over the top of the hill and enjoy the final descent back to your car.

Summary

If you're after something pleasant and gentle with easy scenery and a seaside ambience then this is a ride for you. There is little ascent on this ride and although you go along lovely earthy singletrack through the beautiful beech woods and bluebells of Fleet Forest, at no point does this ride ever get hard or technical.

Start your ride with morning coffee at the Murray Arms, take ice cream at the Cream o Galloway, half way round, sit on the beach at Sandgreen and finish your day with more tea as you return to Gatehouse of Fleet.

And if 18 km sounds a bit much to you, this is a route that can easily be split into two separate shorter loops. You could do a short loop around waymarked singletrack on hard packed dirt paths around Fleet Woods or a simple out and back to Sandgreen along

Murray Arms Gatehouse

Family

Moderate

18 km

280 m

2 - 3 hrs

Explorer 312

Cally Mains Drive. Whatever your choice you are sure to enjoy the tranquillity and lushness of the beech woods, seaside views and gentle tracks.

Getting There

Gatehouse of Fleet is situated just off the A75 about half way between Newton Stewart and Castle Douglas. The ride starts at the Murray Arms Hotel which is situated just next to the Clock Tower on the High St. There is parking in front of the hotel or just down the street besides it.

Start Point

Start at the Murray Arms Hotel and by turn off the High Street up Ann Street continuing up besides the Murray Arms and past the Masonic Arms. What appears to be a dead end road takes you between large stone gate posts and onto the gravelled 'Cally Mains Drive'.

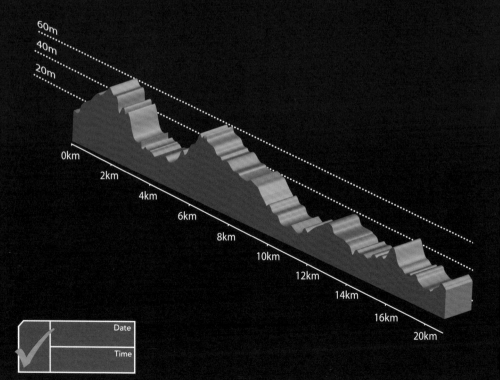

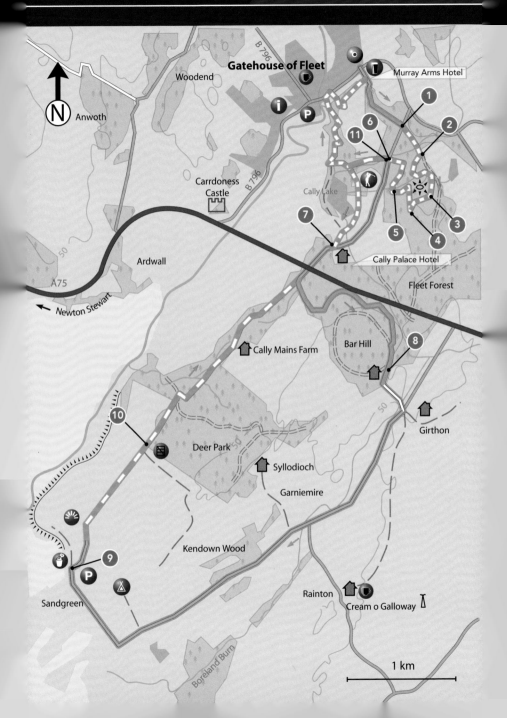

N

Anwoth

Woodend

Gatehouse of Fleet

Murray Arms Hotel

Carrdoness
Castle

Cally Lake

①
②
⑥
⑪
③
⑤
④

Ardwall

A75

← Newton Stewart

⑦

Cally Palace Hotel

Fleet Forest

Cally Mains Farm

Bar Hill

⑧

Girthon

⑩

Deer Park

Syllodioch

Garniemire

Kendown Wood

⑨

Sandgreen

Rainton

Cream o Galloway

Boreland Burn

1 km

XC Route Description

Go along Cally Mains Drive until you meet a small tarmac lane crossing your path. Cross this and just in front of you are post markers for the three trails in these woods.

1 Post Markers

Follow the yellow, blue and white post marker rightwards, going slightly uphill on a brown earthy path. Pass the track to 'Robbers Gate' and drop down to a small bridge.

2 Bridge

After the bridge, follow the path down to a track and at a fork follow the white and blue markers on the right.

3 Motte

At a split in the trail by the information board for the Motte follow the white markers to the left down the leafy trail and keep following the white markers all the way up to your high point and the picnic tables at Cow Park.

4 Viewpoint

Enjoy the rest and the distant mountain views glimpsed through the broad leafy beeches and then follow the trail round to the left, heading steeply down. Take care here as for a short distance the path is very steep. Watch out for walkers coming up the hill!

5 5 Way Junction

After the descent from Cow Park the path levels off and in the spring, this part of the woods is a striking carpet of bluebells. Suddenly the path arrives at a five way junction with a bridleway sign to the right. Go left and down to the tarmac lane.

6 Tarmac Lane

Just opposite you are a wide track and a sign for the Cricket Ground. Go down this track towards the Cricket ground and then right at the first junction, over a bridge and then follow the track around to the left.

A hundred metres further on down the track is a post with a yellow arrow. Follow this to go left and onto the golf course.

Watch out for flying balls as you cruise around on the evenly surfaced path. Stay on this until you pop out in front of the Cally Palace Hotel.

7 Cally Palace Hotel

At the Cally Palace Hotel (jacket and tie for dinner), turn right to go through the stone gate posts and follow cycle route 7 along the lane and under the main road. After 200 metres Route 7 leaves the lane and bears left up a track. Follow this to the second track junction.

8 Track Junction

Go straight on and after a short distance arrive at a gate leading to a white cottage. Cycle past the cottage and follow the lane around to the road at Girthon.

At the road, turn right and wander pleasantly along this quiet back water, with your first views of Fleet Bay.

If you fancy ice-creams at the Cream o Galloway, go straight across the road at Girthon and take the track past the old church to Rainton and the Cream o Galloway. After a delicious break, follow the lane back to the road and turn left to continue along the route.

⑨ Sandgreen Caravan Park

The road ends abrubtly at Sandgreen with a small track going through a barrier and down to the beach. Turn right past the phonebox into Sandgreen Caravan Park. Work your way through the Caravan Park by staying on the main trail.

If you want to visit the beach, turn left at the first junction and go down the small path past Crab Cottage and onto a lovely quite sandy beach owned by the Murray Estate. Pay your dues for your use of such a beautiful beach by buying a drink at the Murray Arms at the end of your ride.

At the far end of the Caravan Park, head for the trees and onto the dirt track.

⑩ Track

At the start of the track is a sign saying 'Gatehouse 3 miles'. Follow the track towards Gatehouse, passing the imposing Cally Mains farm on route and stopping at the turn off to the Cricket Grounds again.

⑪ Cricket Grounds

Go left towards the cricket grounds, going right at the fork, then over the bridge and left down the track again. This time, look for the marker post on the right, just before a bridge.

⑫ Marker Post / Yellow arrow

Go right at the post and along the narrowing dirt path. Snake along and over a small footbridge to arrive on a track next to a fancy balustrade bridge. Go straight on, and after just a short distance you pop out unexpectedly at the Tourist Information Centre car park in the middle of the village.

⑬ Gate

Straight away turn right and go through the wooden gate and into the Garries Park playing fields. Go left and follow the edge of the playing fields to pick up a well surfaced path taking you right back to the start and the big stone gate posts of Cally Drive. Turn left and head down the road to your car.

Summary

If you think you've seen the 7stanes at Glentress and the other centres and don't fancy making the trip out west for another dose of the same then you are quite simply WRONG! You need Kirroughtree in your life.

Without wanting to gush too much about it, when the trails were built here they were built so right it's not true. It's taken trail design beyond an art form. They've put together the trails, but they've yet to invent the words to describe how good it all is. 'Awesome flowing techno singletrack' is a rough approximation of what you'll find here, but it doesn't tell the full story. Go ride it, you'll understand.

Kirroughtree
Visitor Centre

Expert

Extreme

31 km

918 m

2.5 - 5 hrs

Landranger 83
7stanes map

Getting There

Kirroughtree Forest is just east of Newton Stewart.

From the East: Take the A75 past Creetown where the road leaves the coast and heads inland. The Visitor Centre is well signposted from the road at Palnure.

From the West/North: Take the A75 and 2 miles past the A712 New Galloway turning, turn left at Palnure. The Visitor Centre is well signposted from here.

Start Point

Kirroughtree Forest Visitor Centre. From the main car park, follow markers at 7stanes sign. All trails initially start along the same track.

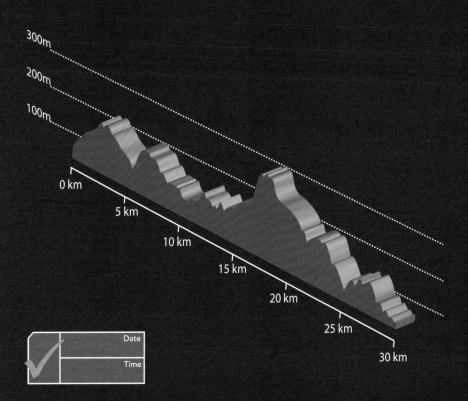

N

176
Larg Hill

Newton Stewart

A75

A712

Bruntis Loch

Auchlannochy Hill

Gleanamour Loch

The White Witch

Rivendell

Hissin

P

3

Palnure Palnure Burn

Bargaly Glen

P

1

Visitor Centre

The Twister

The Jaberwocky

Palnure Burn

Dallash

Stairway to Heaven

Ardwell Hill

Bardrochwood Moor

Crammery Hill
383

1km

XC

Route Description

Here at Kirroughtree there's plenty of rock step ups, slabs to ride up and down, drops to roll or jump and twisting flowing singletrack to rule! And then there's McMoab, a little piece of Utah that ended up in Scotland. You won't find riding like this anywhere else in the UK. It's grippier than you'd expect, but the qualities that make it grippy also make it excellent skin-shredding material, flat pedals and body armour may help to combat the threat of 'trail rash' here.

We heard there's a local bylaw forbidding anyone from riding McMoab without dabbing a foot at least once. Although we weren't able to verify if this was true, it's probably not a law that would get broken too often.

You can get coffee and cake at the Visitor Centre (summer only) and there's even a bike wash there. With more singletrack being added already Kirroughtree promises to get even better, it won't make the loops here any longer but there'll be even more singletrack, which has to be a good thing.

Kirroughtree Black

There's no real navigation required here, it's simply a case of follow the waymarked trails. From the visitor centre car park the trails start at the orange-roofed information panel, and head off from the car park on easy but fun blue graded trails. Things step up a gear onto the Red trails until you reach decision point where you can return to the visitor centre on the Red route or head to the hills on the Black route.

Other Options at Kirroughtree

If you fancy having a go at the black route but don't want to do the full 30km circuit there are a few options you could consider.

Nothing but the Black

Park on the minor road at Bargaly Glen. To get here from Newton Stewart, take the A712 New Galloway road and after 3 miles take the first turning on the right and continue down the minor road for a mile where there's a small parking area. From the car park ride back up the road for 400m to pick up the Red route at the start of the 'Rivendell' singletrack, which soon turns into the Black route, giving an intense 16km loop which includes all of the more technical sections.

McMoab Playtime

There's also parking at the top of the loop at Murray's Monument (Waypoint 2), from here you could go straight up Heartbreak Hill and do the 'Nothing but the Black' loop described above, or just spend a few hours playing at McMoab.

Kirroughtree Chris's Microblast

Fancy a quickie? Too slack for the Black? Then try this.

It packs a lot of singletrack into a short loop, beginning and ending on the Blue, which winds up through the trees at the start and flows and twists its way down at the end. There's nothing technical on the Blue route, but it's a hoot to ride nonetheless. If you decide to rail it around every turn it will certainly focus the mind.

There's more technical Red and Black options as you contour around Larg Hill, with an especially spicy little Slab at the end of this section, but the less adventurous rider can easily bypass these obstacles.

To do the Microblast, head out along the red route as far as the Pyramid shaped monument (Waypoint 3). At this go straight on up the fire road past the Pyramid and after about 100m singletrack goes down right and runs parallel to the fire road back underneath the Pyramid. Take care on this section as it's much tougher than the previous stretch of Red Route and some of the jumps will definitely have you flying through the air. From here it's just pure speed and thrills back to the visitor Centre.

More routes

Whether you've dived off the M74 to head out west or rolled off the ferry in Stranraer you'll be wanting to make the most of your visit to Galloway, so here's a few other rides to explore while you're there.

Glentrool – 'Ungraded' route

Classic 58km Ascent 1200m 5-9 hours

Starting from Glentrool Visitor Centre this fully waymarked trail on forest tracks and minor roads poses no technical challenges. However, don't underestimate a 58km ride with plenty of ups and downs through some of the remoter and more spectacular parts of the Galloway Forest Park.

There's no singletrack on this route, but since it bypasses Kirroughtree you could add some spice by diverting at post 30 and taking a right turn down to the A712, then turning right and taking the minor road on the left after 1km to pick up the Rivendell singletrack. Just make sure you've got enough hours in the day and enough life in your legs.

You'll need to be fit to enjoy this one. The 7stanes literature describes it as "suitable for riders with experience of long days in the saddle" - a bit like the Merrick Circle ride then, but shorter.

Glentrool - Palgowan Loop

Family 14km Ascent 235m

An undulating ride starting from Glentrool Visitor Centre (tea and cakes!) heading north on forest roads to Palgowan and returning on the quite minor road, following national cycle route 7. The route is fully waymarked so just follow the green markers.

Using well surfaced forest roads and tarmac throughout and with no major climbs this makes for a moderate family ride.

Glentrool Blue route

Family 8km

Due for completion in November 2006 this should be in a similair vein to the Kirroughtree Blue route – fun flowing singletrack that should offer plenty of fun for any ability of rider.

Clatteringshaws Loch

Classic 24km Ascent 500m

A great ride for electricity and wildlife fans: Clatteringshaws Loch was created in 1935 to feed the first large scale Hydro-electric power station in Scotland and the woods around here are home to ferrel goats and roe deer.

From the Clatteringshaws Forest Wildlife Centre head down the quiet A712 to pick up the minor road that skirts the west side of the Loch. After the road turns away from the Loch follow it for another 3kms then turn left onto a forest track heading south via Munwhul and Black Loch. Return to the start along the A71.

Introduction

Traveling from one coast to another off road on a bicycle has been a common theme throughout mountain biking since the 80's. Having done various C2Cs in the Highlands, we decided to give the lowlands the same attention and create a new route to complement a new era of mountain biking in the lowlands. Much like Highland routes, our C2C begins in a peaceful seaside setting and quickly escapes into tranquil forests. However this route offers something a little different for the mountain biker.

This C2C incorporates the new face of mountain biking in Scotland i.e. the lowland trail centres. The C2C is a long

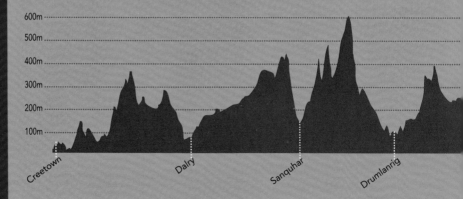

old route and we would need the whole book to describe it in complete detail, so here is an 'edited highlights' version of the route with plenty of hints for extra exploration. Although we've simplified the route in places, don't be fooled into thinking you won't need appropriate OS maps and navigation skills. This is a C2C to add your own touches to, and you'll need careful planning beforehand if you are to complete this in a week.

This 300 km trans-Scotland is split into 6 parts, taking us from the Irish Sea at the mouth of the Solway Firth to the North Sea at the mouth of the Firth of Forth. We've split it according to the towns en route for accommodation purposes.

If you go for the self-sufficient approach, you'll spot bothies, hostels and other options to break up your journey. Add your own flavour to the trip and split it into your own distances - perhaps you'll combine the first three days into two to get going and enjoy more time at the trail centres. Starting in the Galloway hills over to Drumlanrig Castle, you'd be forgiven for thinking you were in the highlands given the rugged scenery.

There are plenty of moments along the whole of this route where civilisation seems more than a few miles away. Choose to rest and be thankful, or spend your spare time taking on the 7stanes .

The Coast to Coast combines tranquility with plenty of adrenaline-infused options. Ridden with the right attitude, this C2C has many rewards, after all - isn't this why mountain bikes were invented?

Sections

Part 1. Creetown to Dalry – 48km

Part 2. Dalry to Sanquhar – 38km

Part 3. Sanquhar to Drumlanrig – 30km

Part 4. Drumlanrig to Moffat – 50km

Part 5. Moffat to Peebles – 60km

Part 6. Peebles to Edinburgh – 72km

Note on maps

We've kept the maps pretty simple as its hard to include too much detail in such a long route. You'll need to pour over the OS maps and work out the exact line (adding in your own touches) and to get a feeling for exactly what challenges to expect en-route.

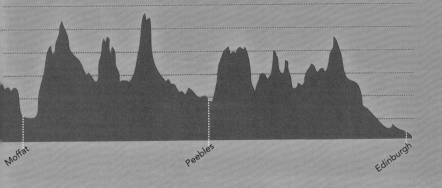

Moffat   Peebles   Edinburgh

Summary

The first day of the C2C shows the contradiction of the route. From Creetown quiet roads and old railway paths meander towards Galloway Forest Park, then once in the forest, the new face of cycling hits you with the Kirroughtree Black run. Renowned as one of the best designed singletrack trails there is, the trail can make you feel like a bike god if you get the flow right. At the end of the outward leg of the black run the trail can then make you feel like a simpleton if you fail to master McMoab's granite challenges.

After Kirroughtree Black run, you experience the oddball of the 7stanes project – the Glentrool trail. Billed as a big day out with big views, the trail winds through the forest park and whilst offering no great technical challenge can hit you with plenty of physical issues. This is a very

Creetown	⦿
Epic	🚴
Some sections of 4	③
48km	➡
1010 m	↗
4-7 hrs	🕐
OS Kandranger 77 & 83	📖

N →

Palnure

River Cree

A75

Creetown

Moneypool Burn

Pulwhat Burn

Cairn of Knockglass

Cairnsmore Burn

Bardrochwc

Kirroughtree Visitor Centre

Bardrochv Moor

Garrocher

2

1

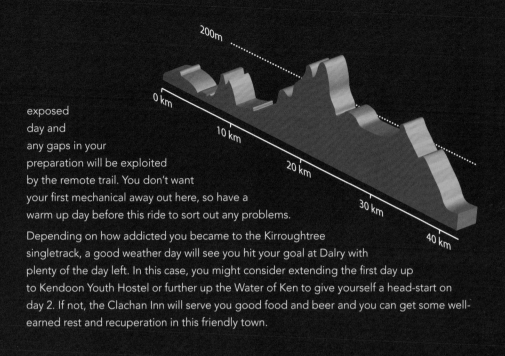

exposed
day and
any gaps in your
preparation will be exploited
by the remote trail. You don't want
your first mechanical away out here, so have a
warm up day before this ride to sort out any problems.

Depending on how addicted you became to the Kirroughtree
singletrack, a good weather day will see you hit your goal at Dalry with
plenty of the day left. In this case, you might consider extending the first day up
to Kendoon Youth Hostel or further up the Water of Ken to give yourself a head-start on
day 2. If not, the Clachan Inn will serve you good food and beer and you can get some well-
earned rest and recuperation in this friendly town.

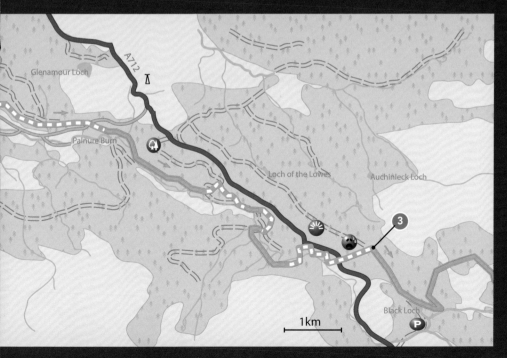

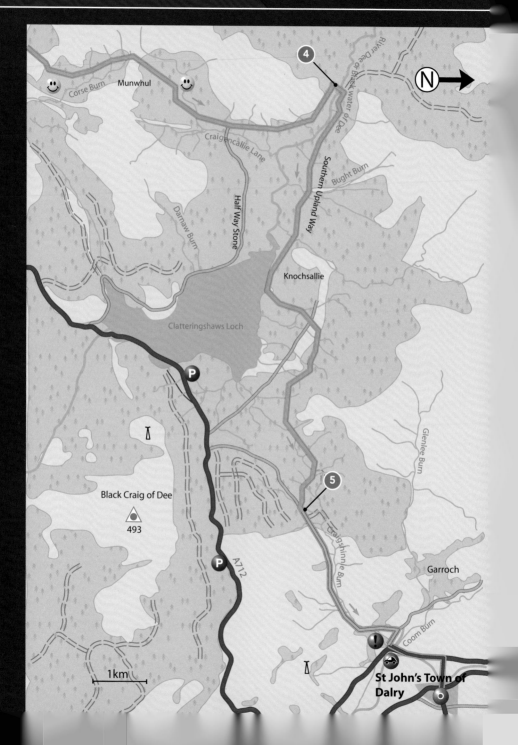

Route Description

1 Creetown

With the Solway Firth to your back at Wigtown Bay, head north out of Creetown on National Cycle Network Route 7. The warm-up pedal takes you on minor roads and the old railway line for almost 10km to Kirroughtree Visitor Centre.

The climb out of Creetown is fairly steep but soon the road flattens out. After 2km look out for a right hand turn through a gate to stay on the 'Route 7' and join the old railway line path. After 4 relaxed kilometres rejoin the road at the Old Carsphairn viaduct and continue to Kirroughtree Visitor Centre.

2 Kirroughtree 7stanes trail

Enjoy some of the twistiest singletrack in Scotland and make your way up the black run to McMoab. This is 15km of some of the finest trails Scotland has, so you'll be glad of the warm-up ride to get here.

The trail follows Palnure Burn northwards, crossing the A712 shortly after McMoab. Test

join the Southern Upland Way and crossing the River Dee.

4 River Dee

A few fairly flat km after the bridge and Clatteringshaws Loch comes into view. Then the SUW turns north and climbs away from Clatteringshaws to the minor road. From here, the SUW follows the road left, whereas we continue northwards straight over the road, gently climbing on the forest road. A further 1.5km on and the forest road begins to descend below the slopes of 'Bennan' to a T-junction on the minor road.

5 Minor Road

Follow the undulating quiet road eastwards towards Dalry. 3.5 km later and you reach a T-junction with the power station on your left. Turn right here and shortly after turn left onto the A762. Pick up signposts for Dalry, following the A road for around 1km before turning right on to the footpath that crosses the Water of Ken in to Dalry.

Summary

The second day of the C2C is a day for relaxing and taking in your surroundings. With less in the way of technical singletrack you may plan to finish day one into this ride and continue on into day three's ride. This section of the Coast to Coast offers plenty of soul rewards as you follow the lochs from Dalry up to the head of the Water of Ken.

Day 2's ride incorporates more gentle gradients than the previous day and you'll find yourself averaging a high speed until you join the forests near Polskeoch. The first half of this ride is easy to get under your belt and the navigational challenge only begins at the top of the Water of Ken where you begin to deal with more 'relaxed' waymarking in comparison to Day One's 7stanes waymarkers.

Dalry Clachan Inn	
Classic	
Difficulty	2
38 km	
710m	
4 - 6 hrs	
OS Landranger 71 & 77	

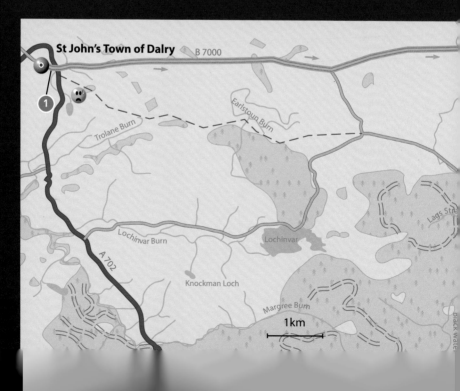

black water

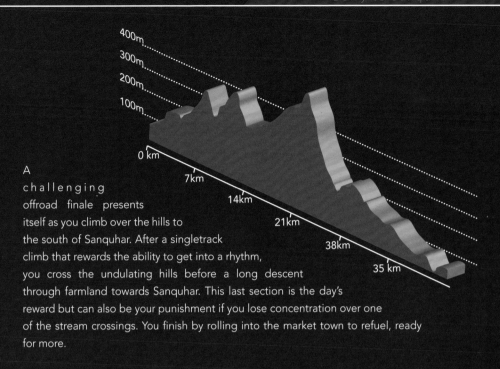

A challenging offroad finale presents itself as you climb over the hills to the south of Sanquhar. After a singletrack climb that rewards the ability to get into a rhythm, you cross the undulating hills before a long descent through farmland towards Sanquhar. This last section is the day's reward but can also be your punishment if you lose concentration over one of the stream crossings. You finish by rolling into the market town to refuel, ready for more.

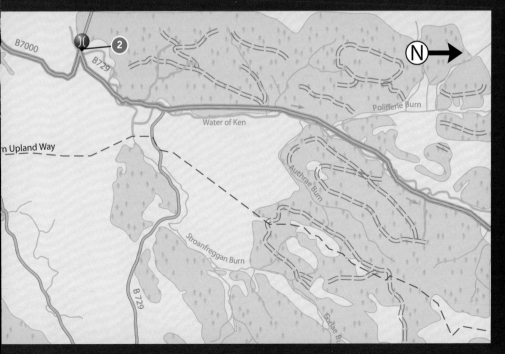

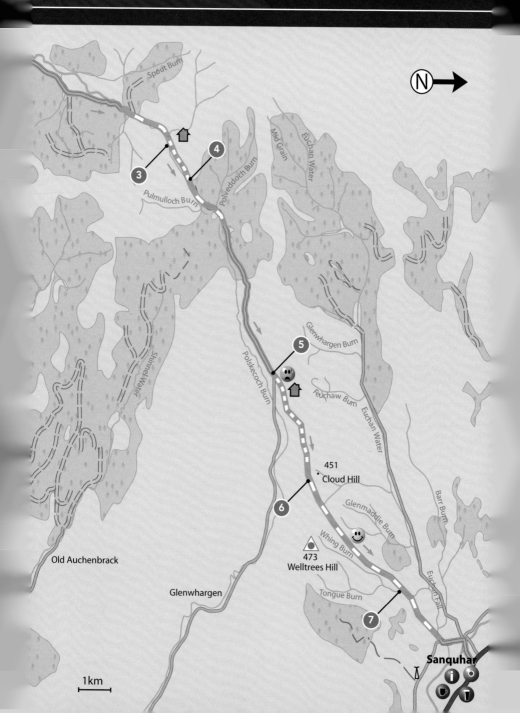

N

Spout Burn

3

4

Pulmulloch Burn

Polveddoch Burn

Mid Grain

Euchan Water

Shinnel Water

5

Glenwhargen Burn

Polskeoch Burn

Feuchaw Burn

Euchan Water

451
Cloud Hill

6

Glenmaddie Burn

Barr Burn

Whing Burn

Old Auchenbrack

473
Welltrees Hill

Glenwhargen

Tongue Burn

Euchan Fall

7

1km

Sanquhar

Route Description

1 Clachan Inn, Dalry

At the junction with the Clachan Inn, head east out of Dalry on the A702. After half a kilometre, turn left on to the B7000, towards Moniaive. This quiet road gently climbs away from Dalry and soon you are looking over the lochs and hills of the Glenkens. Follow the B7000 for nearly 10km passing Kendoon youth hostel, which is run by bike-friendly staff. Another couple of km on and you cross the High Bridge of Ken (take a walk up the stream by the bridge) at the junction with the B729.

2 High Bridge of Ken

After the bridge, turn right on the B729. The road turns from double to single lane and winds its way down to the bridge over the water of Ken. Shortly before another bridge, turn left towards a 'dead-end' sign, and follow the water north. Stay on this scenic road for 10km to the head of the valley to cross yet another bridge over the Ken where the minor road turns to double track and continues for another couple of km to Lorg.

3 Lorg

Once you have crossed the bridge at Lorg, ignore the turn up to Lorg cottage and follow the fenceline straight on towards a waymarker post. The post directs you along the 'Lorg trail' which follows the fenceline towards the forest. The trail is vague but the posts are just frequent enough to keep you on track.

4 Forest boundary

At the forest gate continue as the trail narrows to singletrack. After a kilometre the trail emerges on to a forest road. Turn left to reach a junction with the SUW. Follow this, go right over the bridge and pass the iron bothy at Polskeoch. Here the trail turns back to minor road and undulates along the valley for a few more kilometres before descending a twisty section to Polgown House.

5 Polgown

Follow the well hidden SUW waymarkers. Resist the temptation to follow the farm track leading directly up the hillside, instead climb gradually along the fenceline which points along the valley. The climb can be a little vague and the waymarkers seem to be only just frequent enough to keep your line. Continue this climb for a couple of kilometres until it levels out slightly under the high point at Cloud hill.

6 Cloud Hill

Heading up to Cloud Hill, you lose your view of the valley and rise over the top of the hills. Up here the trail undulates with plenty of sudden dips to keep you concentrating. Finally, you are allowed your descent, a 4km blast that brings Sanquhar closer and closer. The descent, will have you nervously watching your front wheel for dips. Go through a gate and the trail levels out. Follow the fenceline to your right with the cottage in front and descend down to Whing Burn.

7 Whing Burn Bridge

After crossing the burn, the trail rises sharply and then quickly descends again, over a wall, and on through the farmyard. After this, you reach a minor road on the SUW, turn left and follow it into Sanquhar.

Summary

On the face of it this is an easy day, but don't let the lesser distance fool you. The ride from Sanquhar to Drumlanrig can require the energy of a ride twice the length if you are unfortunate enough to have the weather against you.

There are 3 climbs along the way which will test your lactic acid levels, two of which make the most of grass's ability to sap your energy. Half way around, you can sit back and enjoy the fact that apart from the odd hiccup, it'sdownhill all the way now and onwards towards the delights of the Drumlanrig trails.

Fortunately nobody who rides this trail ever remembers much about the evil climbs at the   start of the day, and the minute you begin the descent into the Enterkin, all is forgiven and forgotten.

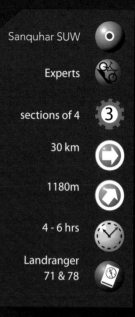

Sanquhar SUW

Experts

sections of 4   **3**

30 km

1180m

4 - 6 hrs

Landranger
71 & 78

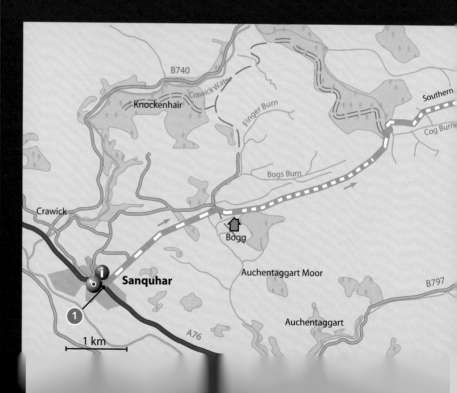

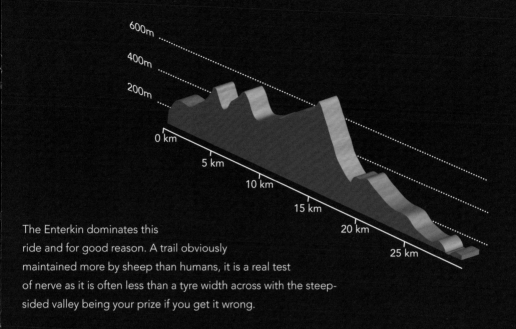

The Enterkin dominates this ride and for good reason. A trail obviously maintained more by sheep than humans, it is a real test of nerve as it is often less than a tyre width across with the steep-sided valley being your prize if you get it wrong.

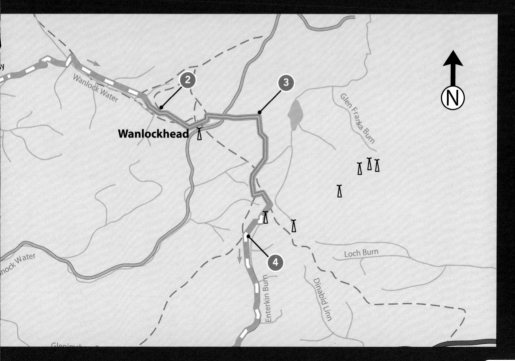

(A) Route Description

Much of this day follows the 2nd half of the 'Lowther Mission' and more info can be found in the full Lowther Mission description.

(1) Sanquhar

After stocking up with all the munchies that you are going to need just to keep you going until you reach the café half way round the ride, it'stime to get going. If you want to stick to the rough stuff, the Southern Upland Way heads north out of the town from half way along the high street, up 'Cow's Wynd'!

If you want to save the energy-sucking terrain until later, take the minor road which heads north out of Sanquhar, meeting the SUW at Lochurn Bridge, 3 km northeast of the town. At the pessimistically named, Bogg Cottage, you are on to the Southern upland Way (SUW), and you follow this all the way to Wanlockhead. This part of the ride gives you two energy-sapping grassy climbs rewarded by two speedy descents. Make sure you fly through the stream splash at the end of the second. 'It would be rude not to'.

(2) Wanlockhead

Heading down the valley towards Britain's highest village, you pass through ruined 18th century lead mines which are reflected in a lot of the local place names. After the previous hairy descent, take the time to wind down and soak in your surroundings on the cruise into

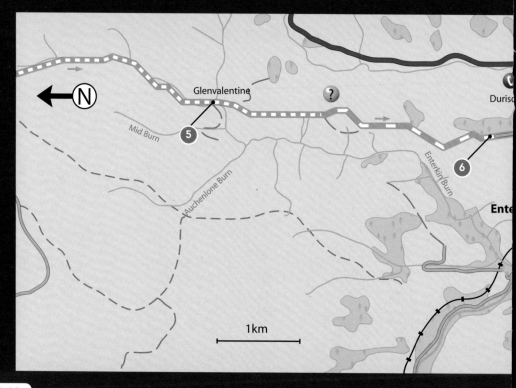

the village. As you hit the main road through the village, cross over to the Mining museum café and enjoy some good food.

③ Lowther Hill

If your legs are under you, the aerial access road is a great way to gain height on your way to enjoying the Enterkin. You can ride the SUW up here, but we prefer to take the road for efficiency. If you have the weather on your side, you'll enjoy great views at the top.

④ The Enterkin Pass

This is the point where the previous half of the ride becomes irrelevant and you are rewarded by a mammoth singletrack descent requiring immense concentration. Enjoy, but stop occasionally to take in the surroundings.

⑤ Glenvalentine

The end of the Enterkin and a little work lies ahead navigating through farmland to continue your descent to Drumlanrig. Ensure you don't spook livestock on your way through as they probably don't realise what a nice person you are and tend to panic when they see what a lovely bike you're riding.

⑥ Tarmac Again

Now is the chance to warm down on the minor roads to Drumlanrig. If you are planning to stay in Thornhill, follow the river Nith south for a few miles, preferably on more minor roads than the A76.

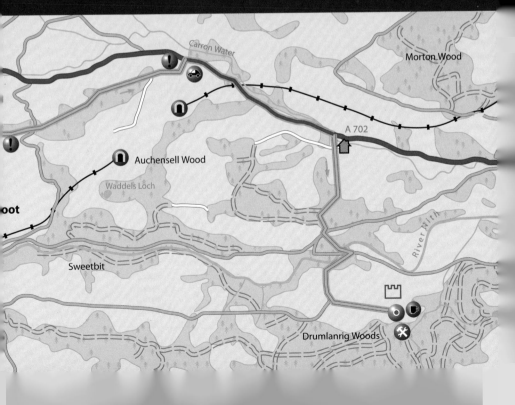

Summary

The hardest part of this day is the start – just try pulling yourself away from Rik's groomed trails (or the café) at Drumlanrig. At Drumlanrig, you'll see all that has gone on to create flowing natural-feeling trails. At Ae, you'll see the face of trailbuilding when diggers are let loose in a forest!

From Durisdeer, Glenaggart sends you into tranquil hillsides and within an hour you feel like you're miles from anywhere. On the second half of the ride, Ae forest swallows you up and you can easily spend an hour at a respectable speed eating up forest road on this part of the journey. Once you escape from the forest, the ride still has a little surprise up it'ssleeve with the 'crooked road' which twists it'sway down towards the market town below.

Drumlanrig Castle	
Epic	
Hard	3
50 km	
1240m	
4 - 7 hrs	
Landranger 78	

(A) Route Description

1 Drumlanrig Castle

There can't be many nicer places to start a ride. If you've opted to stay in nearby Thornhill overnight, then you'll find your way on to the route via the back roads which trace the line of the A76. From Drumlanrig, cross the River Nith and climb up to cross the A76, retracing the route in from the previous section.

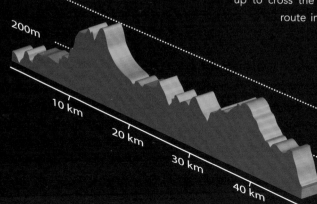

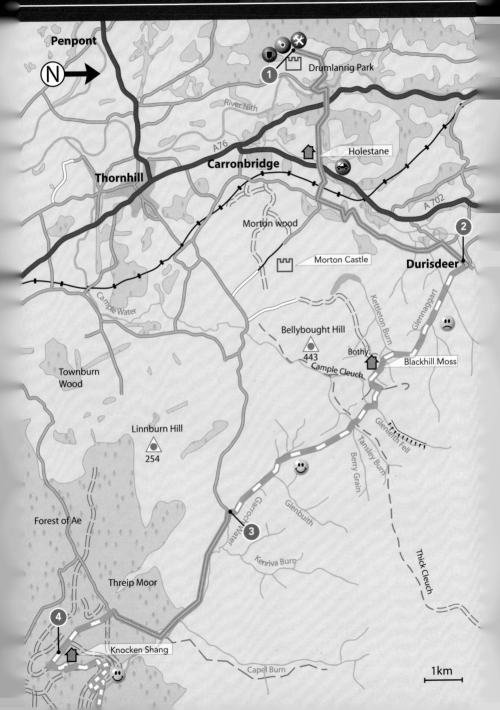

Penpont

N →

Drumlanrig Park

1

River Nith

A76

Holestane

Carronbridge

Thornhill

A702

Morton wood

Durisdeer

2

Morton Castle

Kettleton Burn

Glennaggart

Cample Water

Bellybought Hill

443

Bothy

Blackhill Moss

Cample Cleuch

Townburn
Wood

Glenleith Fell

Linnburn Hill

254

Tansley Burn

Berry Grain

Garroch Water

Glenbuith

Forest of Ae

3

Kenriva Burn

Thick Cleuch

Threip Moor

4

Knocken Shang

Capel Burn

1km

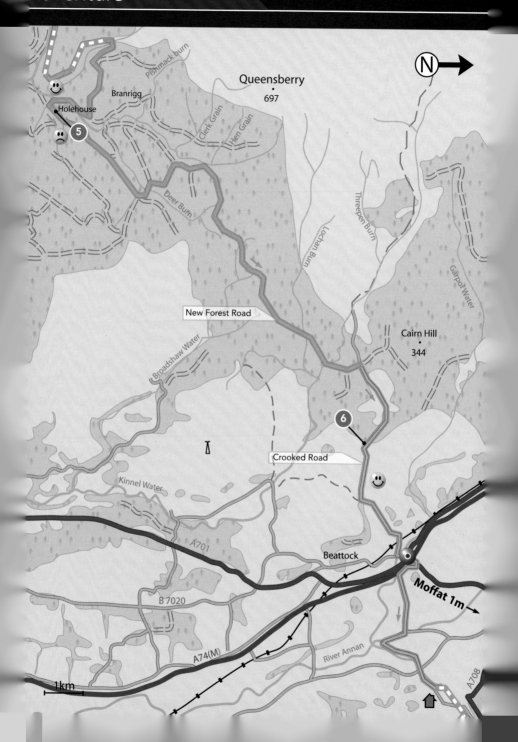

This time, cross straight over the A702 carefully and climb up over the railway line to the junction, less than 1 km away. Take the first sharp left hand turn and continue along the minor road for nearly 5 km until you reach a crossroads. Turn right at the crossroads to Durisdeer.

2 Durisdeer

Before you enter Durisdeer, there is a trail leading away from the cemetery into Glenaggart. Following this for a few km, you are quickly lost in the hills and the sense of remoteness returns. Continue up to the bothy at Blackhill Moss. Head SE for 0.5 km along the valley floor, before turning N towards the towering hillside. Before you begin ascending the hill, turn right and follow the main track SE towards Garroch water. After 2 km of climbing, the trail levels out and then descends rapidly to the floor of Garroch water. Follow the valley floor for a further 2km to a minor road.

3 Road to Ae

Turn left and follow the peaceful road adjoining the line of Capel Water, east past a couple of settlements. Soon the road is surrounded by forest and after 1km in the forest cross a bridge over a stream. Shortly after this the road bends sharply to the right where you leave tarmac and enter the forest. Set off on forest road, taking the right fork to weave through Ae for 2km. After this, you see Knockenshang cottage on your left. Turn left on the forest road to pass the cottage.

4 Knockenshang

At the T-junction after the cottage, turn left to join the Ae 7stanes trail. From here you soon disappear into the trees through some sweet singletrack before being spat out into whistler-inspired tabletops and berms. This trail is a serious 'make or brake' experience and demands respect. The trail drops down to a bridge over Capel Water after the freeride zone, and then climbs back up harshly, leveling out at 'The Face'. Follow the 7stanes trail up and around the forest roads and singletrack, past Bran Burn and around to 'The Edge' – try not to look down! After The Edge, the singletrack re-enters the forest and descends to the Water of Ae, crossing over the bridge.

5 Water of Ae

Continue on the Ae 7stanes trail as it climbs the forest road north. After 1 km, the trail turns right to approach its triumphant finale at the 'Omega Man'. To continue on the C2C route, follow the forest road north, ignoring the 7stanes turn off. After a couple of kilometres reach an off-set crossroads, take the left hand trail being careful not to carry straight on ahead. Stay on forest road, ignoring all turn offs both left and right, until almost 10km later you'll find yourself emerging onto a minor road.

6 Crooked Road

Turn right on the road and continue through the forest clearing and out of the forest. You have now rejoined the SUW and can follow it down the 'Crooked Road' towards Moffat. The road descends sharply after it has twisted its way away from Ae and the road levels out. At the T-junction, turn left away from Beattock and continue to the roundabout with care, next to the motorway. To continue to Moffat, cross over both roundabouts and follow the A701 for 2km.

Summary

The C2C passes just south of Moffat, but if you've gone for one of the friendly B&Bs or Inns in Moffat, you can rejoin the route by following the A708 for 3km until you reach forest and descend right to track back onto the Southern Upland Way.

On this stage of the C2C, the trail seems to split itself into two very distinct types of track, the kind that gives you a lot of distance for your energy, and the kind that doesn't. The energy sapping kind is very weather dependent. Ride it during a sunny spell and you'll eat up the miles but ride it on a howling wet day and you'll wonder why Peebles looks further and further away on your map.

M74 Underpass	
Epic	
Sections of 3	②
60 km	
1765m	
5 - 8 hrs	
Landranger 73 & 78	

There are 3 distinct sections to this day's ride. Start with the forest ascent from Moffat up to Ettrick Head where you feel miles away from anywhere on its knife-edge singletrack. After a speedy cruise down a beautiful country road, there is the up-and-over to Tibbie Shiels Inn for a well-earned dinner. Finally, the ascent over Foulbrig leaves another beautiful cruise down the remote Manor Valley towards Peebles. This is a day for taking in the gentle scenery and getting away from the bustle. Give yourself plenty of time to complete the ride and enjoy a slower pace

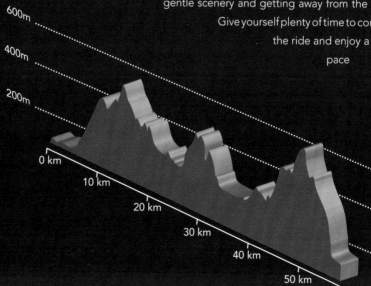

N

BEATTOCK

MOFFAT

Eskdalemuir Forest

B 700

Cornal Burn

Moffat Dale

A 701

Selcoth Burn

3

Phawhope Bothy

Longhope Burn

Moffat Water

Blackhope burn

Southern Upland Way

Kirkhope Burn

Brockhope Burn

Black grain

Cossershill Burn

A 708

Carrifran Burn

Emblem Brae

4

Loch Skeen

Fruid Resr

Loch of the Lowes

Talla Resr

5

Megget Resr

A 701

St Mary's Loch

1 km

N

B 709

St Mary's Loch

Megget Water

Megget Resr

Craigierig Burn

Cramalt Burn

A 708

Farm

Glengaber Burn

Kirkstead Burn

Dryhope Burn

Foulbrig

Whitehope Burn

Craighope Burn

Douglas Burn

817

Manor head

Dollar Law

675 ·

Blackhouse Heights

6

Horse Hope
Hill ·

502

Kill Burn

Stob Law

676

Glensax Burn

528 ·

Canada Hill

Hall Manor Woods

Waddenshope Burn

Cardrona
Forest

Manor water

B 7062

B 712

Cademuir
Plantation

A 72

R Tweed

PEEBLES

Glentress
Forest

A 703

1km

Route Description

1 M74 Underpass

Head back towards the start of the 'Crooked Road' on the previous days ride. At the main road cross the roundabout and go under the motorway. At the next roundabout turn right and rejoin the SUW. After 1km cross a stream and the SUW continues up and over the unrideable hill in front. To cheat (and why not?) turn right and follow the road around the hill, rejoining the SUW on the other side. From here on, stay on the SUW with its yellow markers all the way to Tibbie Shiels. After the riverside section (or cheat again and stay on the B-road), follow SUW signs south-east towards Cornal Burn.

2 Cornal Burn

Follow the steadily climbing forest road alongside Cornal burn for around 6km. There is a short, fast descent leading into a right hairpin bend. On the outside of this corner is the start of the SUW singletrack heading north – Don't miss it! After just over 1km of singletrack, follow the fence line and exit the forest. Pass the sheep pen and ascend along the knife-edge singletrack, you're rewarded with great views of the craggy glens and a real sense of being away from it all. Take care on the steep side-slopes and cross the stream, climbing towards Ettrick Head.

3 Ettrick Head

At the source of the Ettrick, you re-enter the forest and descend a short section of technical singletrack towards the main forest road. Again, following SUW signposts, you lose your height towards Phawhope Bothy. Around 1km

after the bothy you join the minor road which speeds you along the Ettrick water almost 10km to Scabcleugh. If you are doing well with time, there are plenty of scenic spots for a picnic along here.

4 Scabcleugh

Follow Scabcleugh burn up the valley, and climb gradually for around 4km to the saddle. Resist the temptation to short-cut down to Loch of the Lowes. Instead continue along the last short ascent and follow the SUW with its short, sharp descents and climbs around the back of the forest before descending down to Tibbie Shiels.

5 Tibbie Shiels

Cross the lochs and turn right onto the A708, following it carefully for 3km until taking the left hand turn onto the minor road that goes past Megget reservoir. Follow the minor road until the head of Megget and look for the right hand turn by the farm. Follow this long undulating climb across 'Foulbrig' for 4km until you start the fast descent into Manorhead. Buckle up for a 1km blast that gets rid of those pesky contours you've managed to build up and leaves you in a hidden gem of a glen.

6 Manor Head

Take in the seclusion of this remote glen before cruising down the minor road for 10km towards Cademuir. From here, you can pick up signs for Peebles to follow a minor road around the south side of Cademuir.

Summary

The final leg of the C2C is a long day taking you from Glentress over to the Pentland Hills and into Edinburgh along the water of Leith. As the crow flies Edinburgh is only 35km away, but our route doubles this distance to stay away from the traffic and take in some awesome mountain biking terrain.

Dropping out of the back of Glentress, you can tell where the Forestry Commission Scotland land ends and lesser-used trails begin. This is a serene part of the forest which obviously sees more deer than humans. Before you know it you lose your height and begin to climb again through an equally tranquil setting, over Cloich Forest to West Linton. Once you have completed the climb up and over the Pentlands, there is a long triumphant cruise down Edinburgh's waterways and cyclepaths to the port of Leith.

Janet's Brae Glentress	◉
Epic	🚵
sections of 4	③
72 km	➡
1730m	➚
7 - 10 hrs	⏰
Landranger 66, 72, 73	📖

Ⓐ Route Description

① Janet's Brae

Follow the A72 west out of Peebles until just before the 30mph zone finishes. Turn left here following 'Bronze Foundry' signs. Shortly after there is a Forestry Commission sign sending you up 'Janet's Brae'.

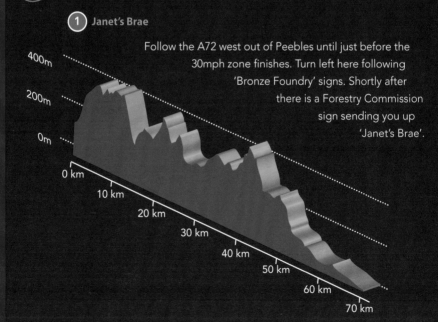

N

Glentress Forest

Portmore Loch

Active farming warning!

Eddleston

Peebles

Eddleston Water

A 703

Kidston Farm

B 712

Cloich Forest

Wether Law

479

446
Hag Law

Romannobridge

Lyne Water

B 7059

A 72

A 701

Dead Burn

B 7059

West Linton

A 702

1km

R.Tweed

A 72

This is an unrelenting, twisting forest road climb that takes you past the skills loop in Glentress Forest, to the Buzzard's Nest Car Park. From the Buzzard's Nest, follow the 'V rail' Black run via 'Soor Plooms' to 'The Tower Ride'. After this short steep climb the Black run crosses over a forest road (7stanes post no. 65) and carries on up to the top of Shieldgreen Kipps. Turn left on the forest road before the climb continues and follow the forest road as it becomes less distinct.

2 Glentress Boundary

Follow forest road all the way until you reach a wall and fence denoting the boundary of Forestry land. Cross the wall at the gap and join the forest road on the other side. Follow the same direction on the forest road as it contours around the valley. Again, continue along the forest road as it emerges from the forest and descends through active farmland. Be aware that a responsible riding attitude is now required, as there are plenty of ways to get yourself into trouble on this descent if your brain is switched off.

3 Nether Kidston

Cross straight over the main road and join the road which descends and crosses a bridge. Follow this as it breaks up and becomes a rough farm path climbing through gates and straight on past cottages. The track rises and then descends sharply to the right to cross a stream at a wooden bridge. You are now on the 'Tweed Trails' which direct you over to West Linton. Follow the distinct path as it twists through farmland up to the B road. Then follow the road right as it descends and take the sharp left turn with more Tweed way-markers. Follow the markers to Cloich Forest.

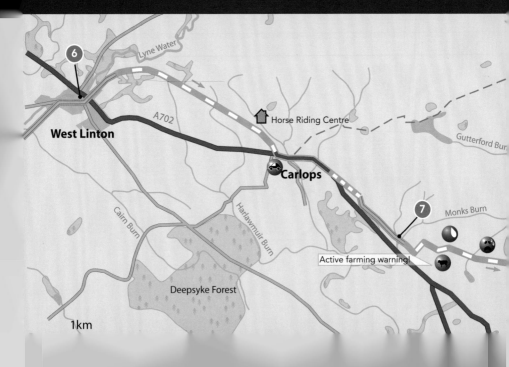

4 Cloich Forest

Once again you are following Tweed Trail markers towards West Linton. The path climbs steeply into the forest and peaks before throwing away the height again fairly quickly. Reach a complicated set of junctions, and follow the edge of the forest to descend in a westerly direction. The OS maps of this forest are misleading due to the extensive logging in recent years. Look out for the right hand turn, signposted, which descends to a tricky stream crossing before descending again to another crossing. From here contour around Green Knowe and cross the Fingland Burn climbing towards the strip of trees to the north-west.

5 Descent to Romanno Farm

As you enter the trees, the trail levels out, and here begins a fast doubletrack descent. Hang on to the trail for 1km as it sweeps right and then left before descending towards the farmhouse. The track here can be super muddy at times and slicker than you'd think for a fairly wide trail. This descent is a great opportunity to get that 'silly crash' out of you system. Continue past the field on your righ and before you go past the houses at the bottom, go through the gate on your righ and follow the fence on to the tarmac roac When you hit the T-junction turn right and then shortly after left along the minor roac with the gate. After 500m, turn left and cross the busy A701, following the B7059 for 4km tc West Linton.

6 West Linton

The B road enters West Linton, past the nice wee café on your left. Follow the winding roac through the centre of the town, up to the A702 next to the Gordon Arms. Opposite the Inn is a

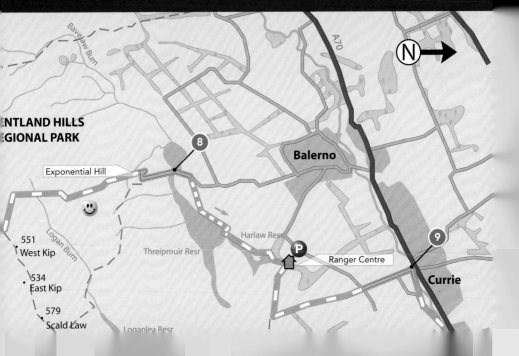

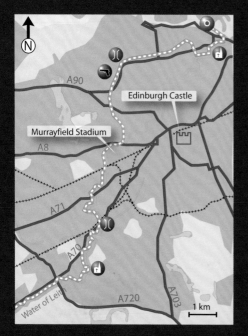

Edinburgh Castle

Murrayfield Stadium

Water of Leith

1 km

minor road leading away from the town. After 1km glance on to a T-junction and continue to your right, following the line of the old Roman road past the horse riding centre back to the A702. Follow the road with care through Carlops until you see the sign for Nine Mile Burn. Follow the singletrack as it widens into double track and further in to a minor road. two kilometres later and you're at the Nine Mile Burn.

7 Nine Mile Burn

Follow the path signs north around the edges of the farmer's fields (keep the faith as it gets a little vague) towards the five peaks of the Pentlands. The trails dips through a stream and rises steeply through a saddle before turning west along the right hand side of some trees to the western side of the five peaks. Passing West Kip on your right, descend gradually

leads you into a fast descent. Almost two fas kilometres later and you'll cross through a gate and hit the road. Take a quick right/left before descending Exponential Hill (look out for the singletrack on the left of the road).

8 Threipmuir Reservoir

Shortly after the road crosses the reservoir turn right onto the singletrack that winds alongside the reservoir. From here, keep Threipmuir and Harlaw reservoirs on your righ and continue to the Ranger Centre. After this follow the path with trees on your left until you reach the car park, turn right back towards the Pentlands and as the path forks, head Eas up the gradual climb. After 500m, turn lef towards the line of trees, descending towards Edinburgh in the distance. Enjoy the cheek bit of singletrack through the trees before you hit the road. Descend for 1km to reach the water of Leith.

9 Water of Leith to the Port of Leith

The river takes you into the heart of Edinburgh Follow the path beside the river for ove 5km, and cross under the canal aqueduct From here, the path crosses roads and parks occasionally, but stick with the 'Water of Leith walkway' signs and dodge the city types al the way to Murrayfield sports stadium. To dip your wheels in the sea, pass the north side of the stadium through the side streets and follow signs for the city centre. On the main road into the city centre, after 500m an old railway bridge crosses overhead. Follow the cycleway signposts onto the old railway line and continue north, following signs for Leith After almost 10km of snaking cycleways, you reach the old Port of Leith and finish you

XC

Epic

Acknowledgements

Thanks to our co-writer Iain for opening up his contacts book for us and, Kona for Ali's new Dawg, Steve Dees for his in depth knowledge of the trails at Innerleithen, Thanks to Nic at the Bike Lodge in Innerliethen for his very comfy hospitality and everyone at The Hub in the Forest, Glentress. Karl Bartlett at the FC, Andy Hopkins and Julie Cartner at the 7stanes project for all their help and backing. The Murray Arms Hotel at Gatehouse of Fleet for sumptuous accommodation. Rik at the Bike Shed in Drumlanrig, Clive and his secret singletrack at the Criffel Inn. Chris Ross and his microblast at Kirroughtree, Roddy MacDonald of Nevis Sport for loan of GPS, Pete Laing and his invaluable info for Selkirk and Yair, Stuart Nicholson and the Edinburgh Road Club for help with the Pentlands Section, Tim and the Bike Chain crew for help scouting and checking routes in the Tweed Valley, Sue and Jack Peyton Drumlanrig ride partners; Stan Yau for a very thorough impromptu proof reading; Sue Williams, Jim Savege and Eluned at the Caban for feeding and watering us and keeping us sane in the busy times.

Photos

Paul Bagot, Velda Edmondson, Iain Withers, Tom Gelling, Ali Chant, Sue Williams, Sue Savege

Map Symbols & Icons

i Information	**P** Car Park		**Animals**
Bike Shop			**Risk to Life**
Marked Trail			**Walkers**
Viewpoint			**Gate**
Cafe			**Take Care**
Pub			**Vehicles**
Scenery			**Remote**
Building			**Wall**
Tunnel			**Rocky**
Church/Chapel			**Jumps**
Wet Section			**Drop off**
Golf course			**NS** North Shore
Switchbacks			**?** Faint trail
Bridge			**Gap Jump**
Camping			**Hike a Bike**
Phone Box			**Table Top**
Fun & Games			**Expert**
1 Waypoint			**Epic**
Downhill			**Classic**
Uphill			**Blast**
Strenuous			**1** Easy
Energetic			**2** Moderate
Start			**3** Hard
Finish			**4** Extreme
			5 Off the Scale

Route Sections

— Single Track
— Double Track
— Road
— Forest Track

Trails and Tracks

— Footpath
— Wide Track
— Forest Track

Roads

— Main Road
— Minor Road
— Metalled Track

Other Features

— River
— Railway
— Cliffs

▲ Summit
⊓ Castle

The contour interval is 100m on all maps except those marked otherwise.

The maps used in this guide are based on standard Ordnance Survey mapping. They have been redrawn to highlight the most important information whilst giving mountain bike riders additional detail to help get the most out of a ride. Whilst we have made every effort to include all the relevent information in our maps, there are times when only an OS map will do, particularly for the longer, more remote rides. We recommend that you take a map and compass with you at all times - and know how to use them.